Traveller Children

Children in Charge series
Editor: Mary John
The series concentrates on the theme of children's rights, reflecting the increasing knowledge and research activity in this area. The perspectives of empowerment and of 'voice' run through the series, and the United Nations' Convention on the Rights of the Child is used as a benchmark. The series editor, Mary John, a developmental psychologist by training, is visiting professor at the University of Exeter. Her research and policy advisory work has been with minority rights groups. Her techniques in this work with marginalised groups have ensured that the research itself is a process of social change and individual empowerment.

Children in Charge
The Child's Right to a Fair Hearing
Edited by Mary John
ISBN 1 85302 368 X
Children in Charge 1

Children in Our Charge
The Child's Right to Resources
Edited by Mary John
ISBN 1 85302 369 8
Children in Charge 2

A Charge Against Society
The Child's Right to Protection
Edited by Mary John
ISBN 1 85302 411 2
Children in Charge 3

The Participation Rights of the Child
Rights and Responsibilities in Family and Society
Målfrid Grude Flekkøy & Natalie Hevener Kaufman
ISBN 1 85302 490 2
Children in Charge 4

Children as Citizens
Education for Participation
Edited by Cathie Holden and Nick Clough
ISBN 1 85302 566 6
Children in Charge 5

Educational Citizenship and Independent Learning
Rhys Griffith
ISBN 1 85302 611 5
Children in Charge 6

Children's Rights and Power in a Changing World
Young Citizens Charging Up for a New Century
Mary John
ISBN 1 85302 659 X
Children in Charge 7

Traveller Children

A Voice for Themselves

Cathy Kiddle

Children in Charge 8

Traveller Children
A Voice for Themselves

Cathy Kiddle

Jessica Kingsley Publishers
London and Philadelphia

First published in the United Kingdom in 1999 by
Jessica Kingsley Publishers Ltd,
116 Pentonville Road,
London N1 9JB, England
and
325 Chestnut Street,
Philadelphia, PA 19106, USA.
www.jkp.com

Copyright © 1999 Cathy Kiddle.

Library of Congress Cataloging in Publication Data
Kiddle, Cathy, 1944–
Traveller children : a voice for themselves / Cathy Kiddle.
p. cm. -- (Children in charge ; 8)
Includes bibliographical references and index.
ISBN 1-85302-684-0 (pb : alk. paper)
1. Gypsies--Education--Social aspects. 2. Children of migrant laborers--Education--Social aspects. 3. Gypsies--Social life and customs. 4. Children of migrant laborers--Social life and customs. 5. Gypsies--Services for. 6. Children of migrant laborers--Services for. I. Title. II. Series: Children in charge series ; 8.
LC3503.K53 1999
371.82--dc21
98-42745
CIP

British Library Cataloguing in Publication Data
Kiddle, Catherine
Traveller children : a voice for themselves. - (Children in charge ; 8)
1.Travellers - Education - Great Britain 2.Gypsies - Education - Great Britain
3.Children - Services for - Great Britain
I.Title
371.8'2694'0941

ISBN 1–85302–684–0

Printed and Bound in Great Britain by
Athenaeum Press, Gateshead, Tyne and Wear

Contents

For Peter and Thom

Acknowledgements

Many people have supported, enabled and encouraged me in the writing of this book and I would like to thank them all.

Devon County Council, in particular senior officers within the education department, agreed to my taking twelve months' study leave to review my working practice and renew my energy.

The Elmgrant Trust, The Harold Hyam Wingate Foundation and the Kathleen and Margery Elliott Scholarship Trust gave financial assistance. Betty Jordan of the Scottish Traveller Education Programme offered much encouragement and a commission which allowed me to learn more about the lives of Showpeople.

My teaching colleagues in Devon, Plymouth and Torbay and across the country all have given support, particularly the Devon Consortium Traveller Education Service team who covered my work so capably while I was away.

Especial thanks are due to Mary John, editor of the Children in Charge series who gave me the opportunity to bring together divergent strands of thought for this book in her series and who has provided an enormous amount of practical support and advice throughout its writing.

It would be impossible to acknowledge and appreciate individually all those Travellers – from Gypsy Traveller, Fairground Traveller, Circus Traveller and New Traveller groups – with whom I have worked over the years, for the various contributions they have made, but thanks are due to them all. I would like to single out Tom and Margaret Lee, whose openness, welcome and challenge to work on a joint project brought me into contact with Traveller families in the first place, and Peter Mercer and Willie Reid who have both made constructive comments on particular chapters and engaged in debate with me about the issues in the book over several years. Also special thanks are due to all the other Travellers who have given permission for their experiences to be shared and their words to be quoted. Some have been happy to be identified, others have preferred to remain anonymous.

I would like to thank Sue Davidson, Karen Merkel, Graham Downes and Sam Richards for allowing their experience to be set down. Also Ludo Knaepkens and Arthur Ivatts for reading and commenting on sections of the text. Teachers in Devon schools and members of the Study Skills Group have also been helpful in their comments on individual chapters.

I acknowledge and appreciate the scholarship of all those from whose works I have quoted and trust that I have referenced them correctly. For any errors or omissions I apologise. Thanks to OFSTED for permission to quote from its publications.

Helen Parry has been a helpful and considerate editor at Jessica Kingsley publishers – thanks to her.

Thanks also to Brian and Linda for good advice at the right time.

It may be a cliché to end a list of acknowledgements like this with thanks to one's family, but the level of practical and emotional support that I have received from Peter and Thom whilst writing this book has been way beyond the call of duty.

Preface

I am delighted that Cathy Kiddle has written this important book to be included in the Children in Charge series. For a considerable number of years, although she would be far too modest to admit it, Cathy has been a very significant figure in the field of Traveller Education known both locally, nationally and more recently for work with partners in other countries of Europe. A number of chance developments in her life meant that she came to work and live with Travelling people at close quarters. Her quiet unassuming manner and her genuine concern about the education of Traveller children has won her over the years a level of respect and trust in those communities. She is conscious of this and is at pains in introducing her work to make clear that in no way is she prepared to compromise the warm relationships she has built up with many Travelling families. This is not a book about the private lives of those families, the struggles that they have faced, their resilience, mutual support in the face of regular harassment and discrimination and their tremendous resourcefulness and determination in the protection of their own culture and way of life. Cathy would not presume to give such an account as that story, as she makes very clear, is theirs to tell not hers. Moreover she could not, however close she may have been, explain the meaning of the multifarious experiences that make up the lives of Travelling people as these experiences are unique to them and their perception of the world. It is now more commonly accepted in research work with minority groups that the 'expert' is the member of the group themselves – they are the only proper and natural mediators of their culture and advocates for their own causes. This being the case it is all the more important that the children of such groups develop a sense of their own cultural identity and a confidence about it. This book tells us something of that very process in the case of Traveller children.

This book is about the activities which attempt to ensure the engagement of the Travelling child and the parents of that child in an educational process appropriate to their lives. Cathy argues such a process aims to enable them to become full members of the wider society to which they belong and active participants in the decision-making processes that relate to their own lives. This is not a simple plea for the mindless integration or assimilation of Traveller children within the system but a provocative account of the interactions between parent, teacher and child that have served to define the ways in which within the educational system their particular situation can be recognised, honoured and responded to. It does not place the Traveller children within a framework in which they are regarded as having deficits which need to be met but rather within a much more positive model of working towards and recognising and catering for the aspirations of these children and their parents, aspirations arising within their own proud and historic culture. So this is a very appropriate and important inclusion within the Children in Charge series which concentrates on processes which contribute to the resourcefulness, resilience and self-confidence of this group of tomorrow's citizens.

It also fits very well within concerns about the UN Charter on the Rights of the Child which form a framework for this Series – not only in terms of the participation rights framed by Articles 12 and 13 but also the non-discrimination rights of Article 2 and the rights as in Articles 29 and 30 which outline the child's right to the protection of his/her cultural identity – not assimilation or integration but a celebration and honouring of that cultural identity. This book gives an important insight as to how both these rights for the groups of children discussed can be protected.

Mary John
Series Editor, Children in Charge
October 1998

Introduction

I am more of a teacher than a scholarly writer, so for me to be writing a book about the work I have been doing is a rather odd position to be in that needs some justification both to myself and to the reader. In many ways this book has been 'in my head' for years as I have reflected on my practice, hypothesised about alternative ways of proceeding and simply tried to understand where I have been and what I have been trying to do. Nevertheless to set some of it down is a big step. To be an effective practitioner it is necessary to be aware of one's work set in a context outside the immediate field of operation in order to develop a perspective and it is important to read the current research that relates to it and engage with other practices and experiences. To write, however, whilst important in the evaluation of practice and in enhancing self-knowledge also involves considerable exposure. My original intention was to continue to think about the issues in this book rather than write them down for public consumption.

After twenty years of working as a teacher in the field that has come to be known as Traveller Education, there was a need to stand back from active daily engagement, to reflect on what I had been doing, take stock of what had guided me and consider the future direction that the work should take. It was also time, I thought, to render explicit to myself – and now it seems to others – the significance of locally based work by setting it within a wider frame. The local education authority, for whom I work, agreed to let me have twelve months unpaid study leave. Thanks to support from the Elmgrant Trust, the Harold Hyam Wingate Foundation, the Kathleen and Margery Elliott Scholarship Trust and a commission from the Scottish Traveller Education Project, this was financially possible. My original plan was to concentrate on two strands of work during this time:

- First an oral history research project, interviewing older Traveller people to get a sense of the lives they led in the 1930s and in the Second World War and, with their help, to prepare educational materials to use in schools.

- Second, a programme of reading, thinking and research to consider how Traveller children were faring after nearly thirty years of Traveller Education projects and in the light of this, to draft a development plan charting the best course for future work.

These were my plans but a meeting with Professor Mary John, then Deputy Vice-Chancellor of Exeter University, changed this. Mary put it to me that it would be a pity to engage only in a debate internal to myself and the authority for whom I worked. She persuaded me to bring the strands of my thoughts together into one coherent text which might be published as one of the books in the Children in Charge series of which she is Series Editor. This would engender wider debate which would certainly be more challenging and should ultimately be more productive. Thus persuaded I decided to write, not just to stimulate discussion with others like myself working as specialist advisory support teachers in Traveller Education, but also and more particularly to raise the issues in a general way so as to bring them to all those who are interested in education, children and who work to promote the rights of ethnic and other minority groups. I was provoked too by the introduction written by Jean-Pierre Liégeois in issue 27 of *Interface* magazine, in which he urges that a frank and constructive debate between teachers and parents should take place with both spelling out their agendas. In these pages I write from my own perspective, as a teacher and a non-Traveller, and attempt to understand the perspective of others. I hope that other teachers, parents, Travellers and non-Travellers will respond in their own ways and that the discussion engendered will in the longer term benefit and include Traveller children.

This has been no simple task. Right at the beginning I had to confront one of the central concerns – that of accountability. In writing in the area of any minority group questions always arise as to whom one is accountable, whether one is acting as a self-appointed advocate for the group, the extent to which the view of the outsider can ever be authentic and if such a presentation renders members of the group as objects of study. Accountability is always a sensitive issue in writing and questions are raised about exploitation and the abuse of relationships. This became immediately apparent to me when I started talking to a Traveller woman about what I was doing. Her first and direct response was, 'I suppose you are writing about us'. It was a predictable comment, and focused me on what I was trying to do, as writing about them was certainly no part of my intention. Indeed one of the main arguments of this book is that Traveller children should have the chance to speak for themselves and be facilitated in every way possible to make themselves heard. For too long it has been left to others to describe and categorise them and their communities. I did not intend to write about families or exploit relationships which have been built up with mutual trust over several years. Rather I wanted to stand outside the personalities and try to understand the dynamics of the relationships between teachers and parents.

It is a very important issue for people like me, in fact anyone working with minority groups in a close way. I thought hard and tried to explain to her, and indeed to myself, what I was really trying to do. My starting point was in my own practice; a review of work and an evaluation of its effectiveness was necessary. However, there was a question about the criteria by which effectiveness should be judged. For me it would be the extent to which I was enabling Traveller children to develop into independent learners and, through this, independent people, able to make considered choices, to stand up and speak for themselves and to act as agents in their own lives. Yet, what I might judge as the effectiveness of my practice does not necessarily coincide with what the parents of these children want. So central to my argument and the evaluation of my purposes has been an examination of the interaction between myself and others like me (non-Traveller teachers) and Traveller parents – the discourse between us. Over the last three decades this has been increasing in frequency and intensity and my concern has been, and remains, to consider where this has left the children. It seemed important to explore the effect on the children that this increasing parent/teacher interaction has had. The ways in which children have or have not been able to take part in the discussions and decisions about the best education for them needed further systematic consideration. In Article 12 and 13 of the United Nations Convention on the Rights of the Child is stated the child's right to express a view and have that view taken into account in any matter that concerns them. I wanted to explore whether they have had such a chance, or whether they are being equipped to have a say and what processes have been important in empowering them to take hold of their own education.

My working life and career as a teacher has not been a conventional one. Chance opportunities placed me in circumstances which put pressure on me to look at a number of situations with new eyes and develop perspectives very different from my original understandings and assumptions about the world around me. I started in the north as a teacher who became through work opportunities a Traveller, though I never called myself this or thought of myself as a 'Traveller' at the time. Initially I did not think anything much about living in a caravan – it was simply convenient for the work I was doing with a touring theatre company – until I found myself being treated differently by members of the society in which I had grown up. Suddenly I was treated with suspicion as an 'outsider'. I moved to London, again for work, into a situation in which I was still working as a teacher, now on an action research project, but this time I was living on a site with ethnic Gypsy Travellers. Now I had become a different kind of 'outsider' – an outsider to their 'in' group, having to cope with a completely unfamiliar 'inside', another culture whose thinking and values on education were new to me and which I struggled to grasp. Again, in another transition, I moved across the country to become a peripatetic teacher in the West Country, but this time living in a house, a settled base. I began to work with several separate and distinct families and groups who were Travellers by reason of ethnicity or mobility, sometimes both, and found myself in a different relationship to each of them again.

In this book I have brought together work in several of these different contexts, with the same purpose of considering the parent/teacher/child triangle. Throughout I have been endeavouring to understand the various perspectives, values, expectations, assumptions, wishes, power relationships and the cultural tensions that have been involved between Travellers and non-Travellers, teachers and parents. The exploration of that dynamic forms the centre of this book with a consideration of how it has affected the children who are the concern of both teachers and parents. I have tried also, as far as I have been able, to allow the children's perspective to come through, to look at their relationships with their peer group, their teachers and their parents.

Since the Plowden report in the late 1960s teachers have been encouraging and enabling access to school for Traveller children. Now in the late 1990s educationalists are all talking about 'lifelong learning' and encouraging the take up of opportunities at every age. Sometimes I think that from a Gypsy Traveller perspective this must seem to have an inverted logic. They have always been 'lifelong learners'. Children are socialised into family ways from their earliest moments and a largely self-employed group does not anticipate a fixed retirement age or pension. They have learned what they needed when they needed it, adapted and changed in a multitude of ways as survival has depended on resourcefulness and flexibility. They have often been repressed, oppressed and exploited, but remain their own people with a fierce sense of identity. For some the notion of compulsory schooling for a fixed period must have seemed like an unnecessary and artificial interruption to lifelong learning, of marginal relevance, except for the formal opportunity to gain literacy skills which it provided for families who could not offer this themselves to their children. For others, school has been seen as an opportunity to enrich and extend family education, with the relationship between teachers and parents the crucial factor in making the children's education work for them. Whilst, of course, the quality, content, the context and the purpose of all learning is also important, it is the dynamic of this relationship that can make all the difference to the outcomes for the child. So this is where I feel we have to look for clues as to what is ultimately empowering for Traveller children.

So this book is not about any group – though I feel I have, over the years, come to have a far greater understanding of my own kind, of the society in which I was brought up, quite apart from any knowledge I might have gained about 'other' communities. Rather the book is about the educational consequences of the interaction between groups – their discourse. Inevitably I have had to give some descriptions to set the scene for the case I am arguing, but I hope that it is only in so far as it has been necessary for an understanding by readers who have not previously been familiar with this field of work. I have tried very hard to avoid stereotypes and generalisations. As in other minority groups there are increasingly members of Traveller groups who are writing and speaking for themselves – these are the 'experts', the insiders who speak with authority, authenticity and insightfulness about their experiences. These are the people to read and listen to for information about them.

I have kept centred on the education debate, partly because this is my experience, in order to keep a particular focus and also to keep within a reasonable length for the book. This focus is also appropriate given that the emphasis of the Children in Charge series is on the empowerment of children and how they come to be 'in charge' of their own lives. Certainly accommodation, health and legal issues are all interconnected with and impinge on the availability of access to education for Traveller children. They have been mentioned briefly in setting various contexts as I have worked my way through. I have not gone into the work of other agencies, nor of Gypsy and Traveller associations, voluntary organisations, charities and groups. The enormous amount of good work done by many to fight against the social exclusion of Traveller groups and the factional feuding which has inhibited progress on other occasions are outside the sphere of this book. The book is not about the campaigning politics of Travellers and others although it does attempt to maintain a sensitivity throughout to the general politics of minority rights groups. This is reflected for instance in my concerns about terminology as labelling, classifying and naming people, which is an implicitly political act placing the group at a certain point in existing power relationships.

In putting this contribution to the education debate on paper I have had no option but to enter this minefield of appropriate terminology. Terminology carries with it legacies of various histories, marginalisations, oppressions and is from time to time 'cleaned up' in the interests of the current political correctness, but many of the old tensions and attitudes remain beneath the surface of the new terms. I have attempted to engage as directly and simply as possible with these issues and to avoid using jargon in a loose way which renders the material meaningless.

Having to put names to peoples and groups has been incredibly difficult. In the years in which I have been involved in this work I have seen what has been deemed acceptable terminology shift and change from group to group. The terms in which some groups identify themselves and others can be different from those which others, outside the particular group, use to describe and attempt to classify them. Today, individual families with a similar cultural heritage to one another will identify themselves by different names, each for their own reasons. No terminology is acceptable if it has implicit and explicit pejorative overtones and undertones.

Let me start with myself and the group to which I belong. Teacher is simple enough, but to the Gypsy Traveller groups I am also *Gauje* (variously spelt gaujo, gorgio, gadje etc.) – i.e. not of their group. In the same way to the Fairground Travellers I am a *Flattie*. I would hesitate to use these words to describe myself as they can be used in a disparaging way with varying degrees of scorn, but to acknowledge the differentiation in culture I use *Non-Gypsy* or *Non-Traveller* where such a separation is relevant.

In the context of the relationships that I am exploring, I and others like me are also part of the majority cultural group in our society. I have called this at times *Settled Society* and *Sedentary Society* to emphasise the essential difference in mind set which exists. Even those Traveller families who are resident in houses and have been for some years, still keep the possibility of movement, of nomadism, as part of their make-up. I have also used on occasion the term *Host Society,* which others have employed to describe the dominant cultural group to which I belong, though always with a sense of irony. It has been a rare occasion when I have witnessed attitudes or actions undertaken by my own community towards Traveller groups which have had any of the attributes one would wish to find in a host.

When, as a teacher working with a touring theatre group where this book begins in the early 1970s, I first began to live and travel in a caravan it never occurred to me to think, name or identify myself as belonging to any particular group other than what I had always been. We were simply members of a theatre company who happened to live in caravans for convenience while touring. Some people ignorantly called us 'Gypsies' using the term as one of abuse. We had no such cultural heritage nor ethnic identity, but there was no term then in common use to categorise conveniently the phenomenon which we presented to the society around us. Since that time a considerable number of young people have, for a whole variety of reasons, some positive, some negative, come out from houses and taken to travelling and living on the roads in an assortment of caravans and vehicles. As the numbers grew, so the trend was noticed and the labelling began. 'Hippies', 'Convoy People', 'Peace Convoy', 'New Age Travellers', these were just a few of the early terms that were used to provide a journalistic shorthand when gatherings or confrontations occurred that attracted wide publicity. All these terms have assumed negative connotations and have not been used in this book. However, there are large numbers of young people living on the roads today whose families have never done so before. Increasingly they have children with them and so they have been a part of my work and therefore come into this book. While knowing that these families do not form a consistent or homogeneous group I have been obliged to choose a term to identify them for the purposes of these pages. I use *New Travellers* here as a non-pejorative generally accepted term, though I am aware that the individual families, if they labelled themselves at all, would probably simply identify themselves as *Travellers,* or maybe *Nomads.* I was interested to hear recently young children speaking in a video about their lives saying, 'We're not Travellers or hippies. We're just normal family folk. We just live in a bender' (Children's Society 1998).

The word *Traveller* has become a convenient catch-all term which is not intended to stigmatise and can encompass many different groups. I use it in this book in this way to speak of Travelling peoples in general terms when situations or prejudices that they face are common to all. Individual families from several different groups will sometimes identify themselves as Travellers. Yet some families will choose to identify themselves in other ways precisely to differentiate their group from others. Thus those who own rides and amusements and travel with fairs will call themselves *Showmen* as a precise definition of their own group, the majority of whom belong to the Showmen's Guild and take pride in a distinct identity built up over the century since the Guild's formation. In this book I have used the term Showmen, but also the term *Fairground Traveller* in the same spirit as I use both *New Traveller* and *Circus Traveller* to make some differences of circumstances apparent.

European research and legislation has added an extra layer of complexity to the terminology, partly in attempting to meet the nuances of differences across usages in various community languages. In funding research in the mid 1980s to establish the state of education provision across western Europe for Travelling groups, a distinction was made between *Gypsies* and *Travellers* and *Occupational Travellers*. In this context the groups designated as *Occupational Travellers* were the Circus, Fairground and Bargee families. It is not useful here to speculate on the politics behind the decision to make these two groupings. It must be sufficient to say that in the chapters dealing with Europe when I use the term Occupational Travellers I am referring to all or any of the three groups so described.

I am left with having to choose terms which will be acceptable to describe all those people with an ethnic identity referred to in the European research as *Gypsies* and *Travellers*. To be consistent with other terminology used, I have used *Gypsy Traveller* in many instances to refer to those groups with a cultural and linguistic heritage reaching back 1000 years to Northern India. Current research tells us of many nomadic groups who were part of that westward emigration, including the Romanichals, the Sinti, the Kalderash, etc. It tells us of the diaspora, the shifting and settling, the encounters and intermarriage with other nomadic groups, the impossibility of a single pure strain of 'true Gypsy', a simple definition or a rigid classification. It tells us of enslavement, forced settlement, assimilation and total rejection and genocide, and yet of the survival of peoples who share cultural values within this multifaceted heritage. In many countries of Europe the variations of the word *Gypsy* are loaded with extreme negative associations. In eastern Europe the people who claim this heritage have chosen to call themselves *Roma*. So in the chapters in which I offer a wide European perspective I use this term.

Twenty years ago in England the feeling was the same and the word Gypsy was considered only a pejorative term. *Traveller* was deemed the acceptable word to use. In the same way the nomadic groups of Ireland and Scotland referred to themselves as Travellers or Travelling people, rejecting the negative stereotype of the Tinker. Yet now that the word Traveller has become so widely used, for some it has become debased. There is a new pride in identifying oneself as *Gypsy* – for the ethnic Irish travelling groups, *Minceir*, for the Scots, *Nawken*. However, not all would do this. I asked a woman in her fifties how she would describe herself and her family:

> My father was an old Welsh Romany. He went over to Ireland as a young man and over there he married an Irish Travelling girl. I was

born in Ireland. When I was six the family came back over to Scotland and we travelled a lot there and then we came down to England. I married my husband in England. His family had come over from Ireland too, but his mother had originally been from Wales like my father. My boys have all been born in England so they are English Gypsies. It's simple really.

So to reflect the diversity of groupings, the diversity of attitude and self identification, I have used a variety of different terms through the pages of this book. I hope that each term will be clear in its context. Certainly every term is used with respect; respect for all cultural groups and respect for individuals within groups who choose to identify themselves in particular ways.

I am happy to say that throughout the book the children remain children. It is how their voices come through this tangle of terminology, how they cope with the complexities of the adult interactions, that is my point in writing.

CHAPTER ONE

Setting a Context

I never dreamed what a difference living in a caravan would make, nor did I ever particularly want to live in one. After some years teaching in a variety of jobs there was suddenly an opportunity for me to join a touring theatre company as a teacher/education organiser. The job would involve liaison with schools to explore the educational potential of the shows that were being devised and produced and to discuss the possible involvement of children in some of the activities that went into the creation of an original show. Also there would be some responsibility for organising and implementing an educational programme for the ten children who at that time were touring as part of the company with their parents and did not have regular, easy access to school.

The job was tempting. It would mean I could return to the north of England where I had spent most of my childhood, as the company's base was there, and it seemed to offer a solution to the issue of childcare which my pregnancy was bringing into focus. The theatre company then was made up mainly of families with young children. Both work and childcare were part of everyone's responsibilities and it was not necessary, not even possible, to fragment life into 'work' and 'home' and make the day to day care of children into a problem or an issue of gender tension. In fact the integration of theatre, celebration and ritual into daily life was a central part of the philosophy of the group. The company, with its political agenda of 'access' to the arts, functioned as a tiny, travelling village. The children existed and their needs had to be recognised in every day's programme alongside the needs of the theatre productions. Indeed thinking through the children's requirements and building them into the work was an essential part of the job I would be doing. I would not have to think about maternity leave and then finding a child minder or giving up paid work to be a full-time mother at home. It seemed to offer the best of both worlds. Within the company there was a determination to give the children access to education, but at the same time that education had to be appropriate to the ideology of the group. I would be able to continue to work in a stimulating job, with like-minded people around me, while keeping my child by me and not missing out on all the fascinating early stages of his development. So I took the job.

My husband, Peter, was pleased that I was keen to do the job as it was the offer to him of the role of administrator and fund raiser in the same company which had made the opportunity for me in the first place. He, after some years of teaching literature and theatre in Further and Higher Education, wanted to move to a job where he could be more directly involved in creating theatre events. If I had been unhappy about moving to a situation with less security, much less money, and the prospect of living in a caravan with a baby on the way, it would have been difficult for both of us. As it was, we both felt that the opportunities were too interesting to miss.

It was in 1974 that we bought the caravan, as living in a caravan had become the inevitable next stage. It was the only practical way to keep a reasonable family home together whilst on the move. To us it seemed logical and functional. Like others in the company we purchased a second-hand Showman's wagon, 26ft. long on a four wheel chassis, which was sturdily built and designed as a family home for the whole year round with good heating and plenty of storage space. We bought it from a Scottish show ground couple for whose marriage it had been built twenty-one years before. Due to an accident they had been forced to stop travelling with the fairs and settle down in a flat and they had no place where they could store the wagon. They had refused to sell it to previous enquirers as those potential buyers only wanted a mobile space for business use. As we were intending to keep the wagon as a family home they agreed to let us have it, very sad to see it go, but happy that it would still be lived in properly. It was quite a responsibility and there was a lot to learn about how to live in a caravan for a length of time. I was obliged to become tidy, to put things away, only buy what was necessary and learn to manage water efficiently. Fetching and carrying every drop needed in cans from a standpipe and boiling kettles for every bit of warm water certainly makes you aware of how much you need and how much you have been wasting when taps have been conveniently to hand. I felt that I was becoming a more organised, less materialistic, less wasteful person, and therefore it came as something of a shock when others began to treat me as a pariah.

There is something about seeing someone living in a caravan that provokes a deep gut feeling of resentment and suspicion in many people in our society. When we travelled to a new town to make a show as part of, say, an arts festival, the company had always been commissioned and paid to be a part of whatever civic celebration it was. A place would have been found for us to park the caravans for the duration of the show and arrangements would have been made for our stay with various council departments. This was never easy, as Peter discovered when, as part of his responsibilities, he had to liaise with officials at each new venue. This was when he first learned of the 1960 Public Health Act which forbade the parking of caravans closely together. It was also his first introduction to the Caravan Sites Act which had been passed in 1968, partly to oblige councils to provide sites for Gypsies. He discovered that the Showmen, from whom we had bought our caravan, were specifically excluded from this act – not included in the definition of 'Gypsy'. The Showmen had negotiated separately, through their organisation, the Showmen's Guild, and gained a special exemption certificate allowing them to park when necessary more closely together than was normally permitted in order to present a fair. Council officials were clearly unsure who we were, what category they should put us into and which laws applied to us. Things became slightly easier when Peter, helped through the bureaucratic maze by a friend who was a civil servant, managed to get an exemption certificate for the company. Yet always within an hour of our arrival a police officer would appear to enquire who we were, responding to a call of complaint from a nearby resident. People would gratuitously call out abuse in the street generally suggesting that we were dirty and scrounging off the state. At night bottles and beer cans were frequently thrown at our caravans. I noticed that shopkeepers kept their eyes carefully on me as a potential shoplifter and one day entirely unprovoked a youngish woman spat at me in a supermarket close to our camp.

In 1974 it seemed that almost overnight I had metamorphosed from a respectable, white, middle-class teacher into a reviled outsider simply by living in a caravan. It was bewildering and profoundly shocking to find myself for the first time up against the rough edge of prejudice, to experience directly the daily small (and sometimes large) humiliations so well known to those born into minority ethnic groups, but so rarely felt by a member of the majority community. I felt angry at the ignorance of those who were clearly so ill informed about my situation. Did they think I was a Gypsy?

I thought about it and as the words echoed round my head I listened to them and caught my own deep gut feeling. My knowledge of and acquaintance with Gypsies was non-existent, though Peter was discovering the legal complexities as he had to find sites for the company month by month. Apart from an occasional flower and heather seller coming to the door of my parents' house, I had never met a Gypsy in my life. From that moment I followed two divergent trains of thought, one emotional and one practical. People passing by our caravan settlements in the various towns and cities where we worked clearly thought we were Gypsies, even though we were living in Showmen's caravans, and they were treating us as they thought we deserved. Until our first encounter with the Caravan Sites Act we ourselves had not understood the differences between the travelling groups. This was long before the phrase 'New Age Traveller' had been coined. I began to wonder what Gypsies had done to deserve such treatment, but only came up with the myths and fictions laid down in my own childhood. All that came to mind were the commonplace and contradictory stereotypes of filth and wealth, of the undesirable and the romantic exotic. I had no idea where all these assumptions had come from and I was ashamed that I knew so little, angry at myself and my own community that we did not care to know. I wondered how on earth it would be possible to become informed and was a little fearful of what it might involve.

Practically I thought that maybe Gypsies could inform me about other things. Here was a group who presumably had been coping with the education of their children on the move for generations. They could be a great source of practical advice for our company starting from scratch. There might be government grants for mobile families who could not attend school regularly, for instance to buy books and materials for parents to use or to employ tutors perhaps. There might be all kinds of special arrangements or subsidies of which we could take advantage. My ignorance was total, but Gypsy families would surely know and might be persuaded to tell me if I could only get some introductions. It occurred to me that other groups, service families for instance, had to deal with considerable upheaval and mobility in their lives. There were all sorts of avenues that Peter, who shared the educational responsibility in the theatre company with me alongside his administrative role, and I could investigate and possibly get some advice or support for our work.

After some initial queries it soon became obvious that the special arrangements and considerations for Travelling children which I had naively speculated might be established on a national basis and helpful to the provision that we were trying to make for our own children did not exist in the early 1970s, although the 1944 Education Act (Department of Education and Science 1944) did state that a minimum of 100 days school attendance annually from children whose parents' occupations demanded that they travel would be deemed sufficient. This provision was a protection to families, obliged to travel for work, from unwarranted prosecution. Nothing else was in place as far as we could see. We learned of the existence of two organisations which it seemed worth contacting – the Parents National Education Union (PNEU) and the Advisory Council for the Education of Romanies and Other Travellers (ACERT).

It was a question of where to start. There was suddenly an enormous amount to learn. It seemed that the previous ten years had seen an unprecedented growth in awareness of Gypsy and Traveller issues, particularly those relating to accommodation and education, which until this moment had completely passed me by. There had been a growth too in Gypsies' own determination to assert their rights to have places to stop legally and to a respect for their heritage and culture in which the founding of the Gypsy Council at the end of 1966 had been a focal point. The Gypsy Council's voice was heard loud and clear through Grattan Puxon's *On the Road* (Puxon 1968) which came out via the National Council for Civil Liberties. The lack of legal site accommodation for Gypsy families had become an increasingly contentious issue throughout the 1960s after the Caravan Sites and Control of Development Act (Ministry of Housing and Local Government 1960) forced the closure of many traditional stopping places and the number of evictions increased sharply. The situation was brought to national attention by the campaigning of Norman Dodds, Labour MP for Erith and Crayford, who in 1962 moved into a trailer in Darenth Woods in

Dartford, Kent and went through the eviction in solidarity with the families there. Norman Dodds documented his work in *Gypsies, Didikois and Other Travellers* which was published posthumously (Dodds 1966) and which contributed largely to a subsequent government report, *Gypsies and Other Travellers* (Ministry of Housing and Local Government 1967). This report sought to establish the situation for Gypsies and Travellers as it then was, with sections on the Gypsy population, living conditions and available accommodation, the family, ways of earning a living, attitudes of others towards Gypsies and Travellers and the provision that local authorities were making. The report concluded that immediate and coordinated action should be taken to make legal caravan site accommodation available throughout the country for Gypsy families. The recommendations in the report finally led to the passing of the Caravan Sites Act (Ministry of Housing and Local Government 1968), part 2 of which made it a statutory duty for authorities to make site provision for Gypsy families.

What seemed to have happened was that in the years after the Second World War Gypsies had been obliged to change their occupations. Mass production took away the living that could be made from the selling of craft objects, such as pegs, and the increased mechanisation of agriculture decreased the need for seasonal pickers and farm labouring work. Families began to turn to the collection of scrap metal and other more urban trades for their livings and gradually moved out from the horse-drawn wagons into trailer caravans pulled by vans and pick-up trucks, which enabled the scrap collection and a greater mobility. Some went into houses. As some Gypsies were moving further into urban areas for their work and customers, housing developments were enlarging the towns and cities, destroying many of the traditional camping grounds as they did so. Gypsies and non-Gypsies found themselves forced into closer proximity and confrontations about places to stop became more frequent and hostile. The 1960 Act had made matters worse, by closing other traditional sites.

When the 1968 Caravan Sites Act was passed, it was hoped that it would, over a reasonable period, settle the accommodation issue. The Act laid a legal duty on local authorities to provide enough caravan site pitches for all those Gypsy families who resided in or resorted to the area. A Gypsy was defined for the purposes of the Act as a person of nomadic habit of life, whatever their race or origin. Once an authority had built sufficient sites it could apply for 'designation' – a status which then enabled the authority to move on those who stopped on unauthorised sites. Seven years later, however, the publication of both *Gypsies and Government Policy in England* (Adams *et al.* 1975), with another review of Travellers' attitudes and local authority site provision, and a young Fabian pamphlet – *Gypsies: Where Now?* (Smith 1975), demonstrated that the matter was still far from resolved.

Access to education for Gypsy children had similarly been brought into focus by the Plowden Report (Department of Education and Science 1967) on primary education in which they were identified as 'probably the most deprived group in the country'. An eighteen-month Schools Council Project on the Education of Travelling Children started in 1971 and some years later Chris Reiss, the director of the project, published the results in *Education of Travelling Children* (Reiss 1975). The book offered readers an understanding of the social context for Travelling families and a review of the then current educational access and opportunity together with details of teaching approaches, conclusions and recommendations to rectify the enormous absenteeism of Gypsy Traveller children from school. ACERT, under the Chairmanship of Lady Plowden, also published an education report – *Catch 22 Gypsies* (Ivatts 1975) by ACERT's research and development officer, in which difficulties experienced by housed and settled Gypsy children attending a secondary school were analysed from the perspectives of school, parents and the children themselves. This report seemed to identify huge differences in assumptions, attitudes and expectations which would be hard to reconcile.

We read these books, reports and pamphlets, but the more we read the more questions arose. Here were we, a group of families who had become mobile because of the nature of the work we were doing, choosing to organise our children's education ourselves, whereas it appeared that Gypsy families did not have much choice at all. There seemed to be little access to school without assimilation.

Peter and I decided that we had to follow up some of this information. I was apprehensive about contacting ACERT as I had never met any Gypsy Travellers in my life so far. It was agreed therefore that I would visit the headquarters of the PNEU and Peter would attend a meeting of ACERT that we had heard was about to take place. It turned out that Peter's trip was to have the greater effect. At the ACERT meeting he was introduced to Tom Lee, a Gypsy who was running an organisation called the Romany Guild from his trailer on an official council site in Stratford, East London. At that time, now 1975, ACERT and the Romany Guild were working closely together and developing educational action research projects. In the course of conversation Tom Lee told Peter that he could not stay at the meeting long as he needed to get back to his site to see a relation, who was very distressed having recently given birth to a child with spina bifida. When Peter said that he too had been born with spina bifida, he was immediately invited to go to the site the next day to talk and give some encouragement to the young mother.

On the site in Stratford, Tom Lee discussed the work of the Romany Guild and ACERT in more detail. There was the possibility of money from Adult Literacy funding and the plan was to buy a bus, go to the unofficial sites around London, carry out some adult literacy teaching and write reports about the kind of access the children had to school. They were looking for a suitable vehicle at that moment. There Peter could be helpful and within a few weeks Tom Lee came up to our base in Lancashire to take delivery of the second-hand double decker that Peter had found for him. In our turn we told Tom of the educational work we were doing within the theatre company.

In the months following these meetings we continued to work with the company, organising education for the children as best we could, understanding now that there would be no possibility of participating in some national education provision for children of travelling families. We kept ourselves informed of Gypsy and Traveller issues in any way that we could and made a trip up to Cumbria to attend Appleby Fair. For me it was the first time that I had any real contact with Gypsy Traveller families and experience of their cultural heritage.

Early in 1976 there was a telephone call from Lady Plowden. It appeared that Arthur Ivatts was leaving the position of ACERT's research and development officer to become one of Her Majesty's Inspectors of schools (HMI) and field workers were needed for about six months before a new permanent officer would be appointed. There was a need for workers for the teaching project with the bus and to make an assessment and a report on educational need among children on unofficial sites around London in order to provoke the Inner London Education Authority into making some proper provision. How would we feel about coming down to London to work on the project? Peter telephoned Tom Lee and he urged us to take up the challenge. As he had understood the situation, we were interested to find out about education provision for Gypsy and Traveller children. If we really wanted to understand what was going on in that world we could come down to London for a while, work on the joint ACERT/Romany Guild project and we would certainly see what the situation was. After a good deal of discussion, about Peter doing the job alone and the possibilities of a job share, we agreed to take on the work together in what was to prove on the basis of hindsight a state of considerable naivety.

What we had not been told about was the factional feuding between the various Gypsy and Traveller support organisations, between Gypsy and non-Gypsy representatives of several groups, which was rife at the time causing a series of splits and realignments and a great deal of ill-feeling. Thomas Acton's book *Gypsy Politics and Social Change* (Acton 1974) documents aspects of these conflicts which we were to experience at first hand on picking up the challenge, arranging leave from the theatre company and moving to London. Fortunately for us, because we came straight into this hotbed of infighting with no knowledge of it, or of the personalities involved, we were able to maintain a certain detachment and concentrate on the work we had been asked to do.

In the end it was not just Peter and I and our fourteen-month-old son who moved to London. Three youth workers in their early twenties, former students of Peter, expressed an interest in sharing the work with us. Two of them had

Jewish backgrounds and they had sympathy for the concerns of other minority groups. As the project had been described to us, it seemed as if extra hands would be more than welcome and we estimated that if we continued to live in caravans and lived simply we could all manage for the few months on the money that was available.

The immediate problem was to find a place to park our caravans. Knowing that our Showman's wagon would be far too unwieldy to shift around London, and was not of a type used by Gypsy Traveller families, we had already moved into a smaller trailer but we had no idea of where we might put it. Karen, Graham and Sue, the youth workers, also had to find a site for the trailer which they would share. Tom Lee sorted things out for us; he would move his own trailer to the back of his plot on the Stratford site and Peter and I could pull on the plot beside him. It would be crowded but possible and there was no resident warden on site to object. The others could take their trailer down to Tower Hamlets where a group of English Gypsy families had been tolerated for a few months on a disused piece of road below a flyover. They said that they were willing to let Karen, Graham and Sue stop alongside them while they were there and would help them in anyway they could.

So for the second time within what seemed a very short period I found myself in a completely new and bewildering situation – that of a gauje (non-Gypsy) among Gypsies, a guest in a way on their territory. We were vulnerable strangers within the group, wondering how to behave and how to approach the work we had agreed to do. If we had been anthropologists or sociologists it would have been a wonderful opportunity to engage in participant observation, but we were teachers and youth workers on an action research project with a definite job to do. We only had a few months to complete the tasks and were asked to provide specific outcomes in terms of written reports on our findings.

The bus, which Peter had helped to find, was roughly converted by turning some seats around and putting table tops in between in the manner of a railway carriage. We were to take it to unofficial camping grounds in the east and south London area – Tower Hamlets, Havering, Enfield, Grays – and offer some basic literacy teaching to the adults and to the children, none of whom it seemed were going to school. We were to concentrate on the adults as the funding was for adult literacy, but the by-product was to record the situation that the children were in. While offering some direct practical teaching, which would plainly be only short term and of doubtful value in itself, we should be talking with the parents and children to collect some statistics and attitudes for a report assessing the educational need among this group. ACERT and the Romany Guild would then present the report with other documentation to the Adult Literacy and Basic Skills Unit (ALBSU) and the Department of Education and Science (DES) in the hope that it would encourage the statutory authorities to take responsibility for provision which then was only being undertaken piecemeal by some Local Education Authorities (LEAs) and a few voluntary organisations. Lady Plowden would direct the project and Tom Lee would introduce us to the sites and families and guide and assist us day by day.

It was strange. We had contacted Gypsies in the first place to find out if there was official state help to educate our own children out of school. What we found were families with little choice but to educate their own children out of school with no state help, who were looking to us to help them persuade the state authorities that they should have proper access into school. Access without assimilation, functional literacy, for vehicle documents, road signs and letters, without cultural strings attached was what they seemed to want.

Essentially over the next four months we worked on the project as agreed, sometimes going out with the bus in a group, sometimes visiting smaller sites in ones and twos. The work, as it may be imagined, was stimulating, frustrating, exhausting and eye-opening, leaving me on many occasions shocked and angry, rarely with the Gypsy Traveller families with whom I was becoming acquainted, but most often with people from my own community for the attitudes I saw displayed. What was really catching my interest was the framework within which we were living and working which was challenging all my assumptions and continually provoking questions about what the five of us were doing that I found hard to answer.

The families on the two sites where the five of us plus one toddler were living were constantly questioning us about our domestic and personal arrangements. Peter, I and our son were in one trailer as a family on the official Stratford site. In the other trailer on the unofficial site, Graham and Karen were an unmarried couple and Sue a single woman. The questioning we received was not in any way hostile, but persistent and puzzled as they tried to make sense of our situation from their own perspective. They were doing exactly as we were from our own point of view. I found myself answering what I thought at first were questions with obvious answers, but ones which were gradually revealing a series of different cultural attitudes, assumptions and values from my own.

- Why did I have only one child?
- Why didn't I want any more?
- Why did I go out and teach when my husband could obviously support me?
- Was it not important to spend time keeping my trailer clean?
- Why did my husband allow me to go out working on my own on strange sites where I might be vulnerable?
- Why were we working so far away from our family homes?
- Did our parents not want us working with them?
- Why did we want to live among Gypsies?

- How could Graham, Karen and Sue all share the same trailer?
- Where did they sleep?
- Why did Graham and Karen not want to get married and start a family?
- What did their parents think?
- How many bowls did we have for our washing?
- Why didn't Graham think it was demeaning to wash up?
- What kind of family did Sue have?
- How could they let her work away from home on her own?

I could understand the questions and concern about privacy and washing in a group used to living in confined spaces often with limited access to water and basic facilities. As I lived longer in a trailer myself I could see the sense in having separate bowls for dealing with cooking and washing oneself. The gender based questions came to me sounding strangely old fashioned at a time when the women's liberation movement was in full cry. The ideas of that movement were known to the families through the media, but it was almost as if these ideas were coming from a foreign television network. They did not really touch their lives. I was beginning to have a sense of that distance myself. Living on the site, working with the families day by day, was somehow like being encapsulated in a tiny separate world. I was aware of the 'other' surrounding world as it touched us and we had dealings with it every day, but it did feel increasingly at a distance from where the centre of my attention was and I began to observe some of the habits and actions of my own cultural group with an increasing and often unnerving objectivity.

One day we heard about a fight that had occurred. It seemed that a group of young gauje men had picked on a Gypsy man out on his own. When the news got out a crowd of Gypsies had gone to his aid and a street brawl had ensued. When I asked Tom Lee about it he did not understand why I didn't find it a normal response to such a situation. 'Of course you will help your own kind', he said, 'If you were on your own and you were attacked in the street, your people would protect you wouldn't they?' I certainly wouldn't count on it.

Although we were made welcome on the sites and were plainly doing a job of work, I always felt that we were there as guests. Only once or twice did we have any trouble with families on neighbouring plots, and each time there was an incident, which made it clear to us that we had upset someone, it followed a time when we had invited other friends of our own to visit us. It was as if we were being reminded that the space we occupied was not ours to control, to exploit or treat as if it were our own home. We were being warned against bringing outsiders into a territory that was not our own. Although we were living on the sites we did not belong to the group in any real sense. We were still very much outsiders ourselves, though accepted for the work we were doing and treated for the most part with great hospitality. However, it was clear that we were only there for the work and could not presume to bring our own ways of life to the sites.

To go back to the questions that we were being asked by the Gypsy families, those that pertained to the particular relationship between parents and children and the place of the child within the family were the ones I found most engaging. Some of the Traveller women, looking at Sue's situation, could not understand how parents could be so irresponsible as to let their teenage daughters leave home and live on their own in a society as promiscuous and fraught with moral danger as they perceived ours to be. Similarly they found it hard to understand any young girl wanting to leave the care, protection and love of her family. A family without love, or at least mutually accepted care and responsibility was incomprehensible to them. In fact Sue's family was a loving and caring one in which her parents were delighted that she had taken advantage of the educational opportunities open to her and that she had gone away to college to develop her potential further. They regarded her work in London as proof of the maturity of a capable and independent young woman of whom they were proud.

One or two of the Traveller women, in a way similar to my own, saw their own group's culture from another perspective when they were able to observe closely the situation of the three women in our group. One woman in her late twenties, married with three children, had never been out socially without either her father or her husband in attendance. She said how she would love simply to go to see a film completely alone. Another said how she longed to write a novel: she read in the papers the biased, usually unsympathetic accounts of her way of life and wanted to write of it in her own way. To set the record straight. But she had no time or space to herself in which she could begin to do it. She had no separate identity to develop that could exist outside the demands of the family structure. Within the Gypsy cultural groups it seemed that the children were precious beyond measure, but at the same time the needs of the family as a social and economic unit would take precedence over those of the individuals within it. Children were encouraged and taught to develop in a way which would confirm their place and responsibilities within the family. The interdependence of the family members was a survival strategy within a society which tried alternately and sometimes simultaneously to reject and assimilate them.

I became increasingly aware that the family/child relationships which I saw were fundamentally different from the majority view in our society. The society in which I had grown up gives the highest priority to enabling each individual child to develop its potential to the utmost. This difference in attitude raised basic questions that lay at the core of our educational work. We were seeking to give Gypsy Traveller children access to education provision without really exploring in depth with the parents what they wanted from us for their children.

Never having in the past been able to assume access to the basic educational rights offered to the majority, the parents had maintained and fulfilled the responsibility of educating their children themselves to survive capably in the society in which they found themselves. The strong mutual support of the extended family was a key factor in this. Our work could easily have a colonial flavour to it if we did not take care to work with the parents. Who was responsible for the fact that so many Gypsy Travellers had remained such an identifiably separate group in our society after 500 years, even though others had been assimilated and were now 'hidden'? Did they look at our attitudes and values and keep as great a distance as they could, or did we, the 'host' society with our inability to cope with uncontrolled, independent minded nomadic groups, coupled with a recurring need to find scapegoats at times of social anxiety, deny access and opportunity to those who did not conform? It was as important for us to consider what kind of education, within what culture, we were offering to the families as to enquire from them what they were looking for.

Most important of all we needed to consider where all this exploration and debate would leave the children. Would it be possible for their voices to be heard, their aspirations met, if there was an adult struggle for the power to influence their education in addition to the traditional assumption that their lives would develop in relation to the roles expected of them within their family structure? I only began to be aware of the social and political implications of these questions during my work for ACERT and the Romany Guild in the long hot summer of 1976. (Another question I never had the chance to find an answer to was what everybody did when it rained!)

That was over twenty years ago and it is not my inclination to indulge in nostalgia or write an historical account. Rather, the aim is to look at the position of Travelling children today and see how they have fared in the playing out of this largely adult scenario. During that time I have remained employed and engaged in the field of Traveller Education mainly in the development of a local authority Traveller Education Service, so it is not easy to be objective. However, my intention is to put forward a perspective on what has been going on within the Gypsy/non-Gypsy dynamic and reflect upon it. In the last twenty years the development of education provision has been a dominant factor in Gypsy/non-Gypsy relations. In the words of Jean-Pierre Liégeois:

> going to school is a significant new phenomenon for the present generation of Gypsy and Traveller children. It is a change both in itself – in the fact of making use of an outside institution – and it is also an opening up to the changes that school may bring into the children's lives. (Liégeois 1994, p.88)

and:

Is there currently a convergence between the wishes of Gypsy and Traveller communities and the wishes of surrounding populations? On the one hand Gypsy children, like every other kind of children, reach the age of compulsory school attendance in whatever State they are living in, and the authorities see no reason why they should be exempted. On the other hand, more and more Gypsy families feel that schooling would be of use to their children, and that it is increasingly necessary to enable them to adapt to surrounding societies and to improve their own living conditions. While these motivations are not to be confused, it is nonetheless possible to say that there is a formal convergence between the desire of one to provide schooling and the desire of the other to avail of it. (ibid., p.222)

The aim of this book is to examine the position in which the children find themselves within this convergence – if it really exists – and to see whether their own views and wishes are likely to be squeezed out between two adult sets of motivations, or whether their individual voices can more fully and ably be raised and heard with a mutuality of support coming from either side.

CHAPTER TWO

Travelling Children – Welcome in School?

It is now more than twenty years since I worked on the action research project for ACERT and times have changed. Many, many Gypsy Traveller children are now attending primary schools. Access to school is still not inevitable or assured (and this will be considered in the next chapter), but the children are there in ever increasing numbers. Progress has been slow. When the schools' inspectorate first published a discussion paper on the education of Traveller children (DES 1983) it was estimated that only 40 per cent to 50 per cent of primary aged Traveller children were attending school, and of those very few were attending regularly. By 1996, when the inspectorate, now within The Office for Standards in Education (OFSTED), produced an updated report (OFSTED 1996), primary school attendance had substantially increased. One of the main findings of the OFSTED report was that: 'Considerable progress has been made in the development of positive attitudes and trusting relationships between schools and the different Travelling communities, who, by reason of their nomadic life styles, have traditionally been hindered in their access to education' (OFSTED 1996, p.7).

Yet the same report states:

> Concern is expressed by some TES that even after unbroken participation in primary education, a worrying number of Travelling pupils are still leaving their primary schools at the end of Key Stage 2 with levels of achievement which are well below average national age-related expectations and unsatisfactory for their abilities. (OFSTED 1996, p.17, para.33)

J-P. Liégeois expresses himself somewhat more bluntly, 'Up to now, school provision for Traveller children has been a failure for all concerned' (Liégeois 1994, p.204).

Of course Liégeois is speaking in broad terms of the situation across Europe, but the OFSTED report commenting only on practice in England reveals that many Traveller children even when they do get access to primary schools, fail to reach their potential. The aim of this chapter is to explore this concern and look at the nature of the experience of Traveller children in school in England and at some of the factors which hinder or help them to progress.

That school and home often represent different cultural environments is a commonplace and equally the case for all children whatever their ethnic origin. Many writers and researchers have gone over this terrain looking at issues of language, routines, assumptions and expectations from the points of view of children, families and teachers. 'All children come into school with a unique personal culture, whatever their ethnic origin. As educators we need to affirm and respect what each child brings' (Duncan 1992, p.47).

Each child needs a welcome, help to become familiar with the ways of his/her new teacher, the layout of the classroom and the daily routines of the school, and to be allowed a period to adjust. For some, notably those with a cultural background similar to that of the teacher, it will be easier; for every child it will be different. There can be no generalising, even among Traveller children, for there are several distinct groups of Travellers and a whole spectrum of attitudes and opinions expressed by individual families in each group. Each Traveller family will be at a different state of awareness of education and its opportunities and each set of parents will bring memories of their own school experience (if any) with them. Some Traveller parents will have been to school themselves for longer or shorter periods and have either good or bad memories of the experience, others will not have attended at all. Some will be literate, others not. Some Traveller children may come to school at the age of five from fairly settled accommodation having already had time in a nursery class or a pre-school playgroup. Others may not see the inside of any educational establishment until the age of seven or eight or even older. Some may arrive after a series of brief encounters with other schools in the context of a pattern of evictions or short stops. It may be that because the Traveller children are white and mostly come into school speaking English as their first language, their experience and cultural differences will not be acknowledged or understood. Behaviour not conforming to the standard of the non-Traveller teacher may be considered deliberately disruptive.

Language will be an issue in some cases, for instance among the families travelling with circuses. Circus is an international business and often families from several nationalities will be touring together. Recent Gypsy Traveller asylum seekers coming to England from eastern Europe (where they choose to call themselves Roma) will obviously come with other first languages than English, but some British born Gypsy Travellers will also regularly incorporate Romani words into their spoken English and their usage of some words may differ from standard English.

Whatever the individual differences between Traveller families they all suffer to a greater or lesser degree from negative stereotyping by non-Travellers. We expect all teachers to be professionals and most I suspect would subscribe to the philosophies of education for all and equal opportunities, and yet time and again, when I have telephoned a school to enquire after places for children, I have caught a sudden intake of breath, a slight change in the tone of voice, a new wariness in the conversation when it becomes clear that it is Gypsy Traveller children I am seeking to enrol. I am not speaking of an isolated occurrence, but a reaction I have experienced so many times that I believe that in whatever circumstances those children arrive in school they will have to cope to a certain extent with the burden of accumulated popular fiction and stereotype that comes with being identified as Gypsy.

Each one will be a long way from the stereotype, but Gypsy Traveller children will certainly come into school with a strong sense of family identity. In the introduction to *Language, Culture and Young Children* Pat Pinsent writes: 'The young child's environment, both linguistic and cultural will inevitably have had a considerable effect on their cognitive development, even by the time that they arrive in a nursery school or play group' (Pinsent 1992, p.4).

How much more so will this be the case if the children do not come in contact with an educational institution outside the home until statutory school age or even later. The take up of pre-school educational opportunities by Gypsy Traveller parents for their children is considerably less than the norm for the non-Traveller population for a number of reasons. First there are the same difficulties of access as with access to school which will be examined in detail in the next chapter. Added to this is the comparative scarcity of pre-school places, particularly for mobile families who cannot necessarily predict their arrival in any particular area, nor guarantee a length of stay. Transport and financial difficulties may also be factors affecting access at this stage. Gypsy Traveller parents are highly protective of their young children and this may lead to an unwillingness in many cases to allow the little ones out of the family environment, particularly when they may have little knowledge of or reason to put their trust in the providers of the pre-school place. Family groups who have experienced hostility and marginalisation throughout their lives make a virtue of internal mutual support and will not let the young children go outside the security of the family easily.

Parents, unlikely to have had any structured pre-school experience themselves, may not be convinced of the value of play as an aspect of learning. They may consider activities such as painting, cutting up pieces of paper and card, modelling with junk materials and using glue unnecessary and messy. It is unlikely that even those who are literate will have read early years educational material. Nursery teachers, playgroup leaders or others in liaison roles will often need to discuss the purpose of the sessions and demonstrate the facilities and safety of their premises to parents before the children will be permitted to attend.

Meanwhile learning within the family will be well under way. At home the children will have already embarked on role play and apprenticeship learning within the extended family group. Fran Duncan tells of visiting a Traveller family who were camped by a scrapyard and finding the young children busily playing at sorting metals themselves – 'Children who live in a house will play "houses" so why not "scrapyards" in a scrapyard?' (Duncan 1992, p.47). I had a similar experience when reading a story, which had been composed collaboratively in a reception class by a young Gypsy Traveller girl and two classmates. Their story was of a little girl captured by a wicked witch. She is rescued by her brother Jack and their grandparents and when the witch eventually dies, her castle turned: 'to gold, silver, brass and lead'. 'Brass and lead' had been insisted on by the Traveller girl who was already very familiar with the value of these metals. Fran Duncan also confirms the early development of an understanding of family:

> From an early age Travelling children are told stories relating to their past and quickly develop a feeling for their own roots and culture. They will come into school with a very definite sense of identity, which must be accepted and affirmed for home/school 'bonding' to be established. (Duncan 1992, p.52–53)

When a family of Gypsy Traveller children come into a new school it could be for the younger ones at least their first time outside the family group and they will probably seek the protection of older siblings. Some schools will allow brothers and sisters or close relations to go initially into the same class despite age differences to help the children to settle in and make them feel more comfortable. It is indeed likely that parents will be expecting older siblings to take care of the little ones and the older children in their turn will be used to accepting this responsibility at home. One school, which regularly admits Traveller children on a short stay basis, will suggest that older sisters stay with young siblings in their class for a day or two. Not only are they a comfort and help, but they themselves have the opportunity to reinforce their basic skills in a non-threatening environment. They can then extend their duty of care to the playground where an enforcement of infant/junior segregated areas can otherwise cause distress or seem incomprehensible and unreasonable to the children.

Living in a trailer, as I had discovered myself, brings with it its own attitude to space and notions of the 'inside' and the 'outside'. To begin with, because the actual space inside is so limited, most living and activity takes place outside allowing and engendering interaction between members of the extended family who may be camping together in a group. Thus the children, using the space outside can relate to a number of different trailers and adults, shifting their focus and attention from one to another of the work and leisure activities that will be going on. Children coming new to school will probably never have been indoors for a period as long as a school day before and this may well cause restlessness and the size of the classroom itself will be unnerving.

When I moved back into a house after three years of trailer living, I found the emptiness around me within the walls distinctly strange for a time. I would sit on the sofa in the middle of the room and wonder how to use the space around me, because I was so accustomed to going outside whenever there was something to be done. After a while I began to accumulate possessions again to fill the space up.

Limited storage space in a trailer determines a particular attitude to possessions – they have to have a *raison d'être*. If they are not utilitarian or objects of value in decorative and financial terms – they are unlikely to be kept by Gypsy Travellers for long. Family photographs which are treasured and collected as growing family archives are the exception to the rule. There is minimal space for toys and this can mean that for the children coming into school, 'A classroom can be like an Aladdin's cave – the children will want hands-on experience' (Devon Traveller Education Service 1996).

There is little sentiment in trailer living. I have a clear memory from the days when I lived in a trailer of a Gypsy Traveller woman being mystified as to why I should want to keep a book in my trailer taking up valuable space after I had read it. When we first moved into our caravan Peter and I had had great fun deciding which of our extensive collection of books would come with us. We allowed ourselves twenty each and in the manner of the radio programme *Desert Island Discs* agonised and mused and reminisced over which our chosen few would be. In the event, as I recall it, I rarely touched any of them the whole time we lived on the site in London. It was not from a lack of desire to read, nor the realisation that I had made the wrong selection, nor even a lack of time, but the complete absence of solitude and private time that comes with trailer living. There seemed never any time to be alone. All this of course has implications for the ability of Traveller children to complete homework, or have the opportunity for study at home, quite apart from the fact that parents may not be literate or welcome the encroachment of school into home time. If the parents are not supportive of what is going on in school it will be difficult for the children to do school work at home. Earlier this year I interviewed a seventy year old Gypsy Traveller woman who recalled how irritated her father had been when she tried in the evening to read books that she had brought home from school – 'They won't get you a living, my girl'.

There is another 'inside'/'outside' dynamic at work in Gypsy Traveller culture which can affect a child's early development. The inside of a trailer is often the only space over which the women have any kind of control and which they can call their own to decorate and keep as they choose. Many Traveller women, despite having several young children, knowing that their menfolk are engaged daily in trades such as building and demolition work, scrap collecting or tarmac laying which will inevitably mean getting dirty, and despite having to live in many cases on unauthorised sites with outside conditions of mud and squalor and a shortage of water, nevertheless use laces and satins to furnish their trailers, put up displays of fine porcelain, and take pride in maintaining their homes to the highest of standards. In these circumstances two separate standards of discipline are maintained for the children – inside they will be expected to behave themselves, be respectful, not be brazen and make no mess. Outside they will be free to move about, help with work that is going on with vehicles or animals and materials of all kinds, and play with the other children who are around with whatever materials come to hand. Coming into the trailers the children will remove their shoes and their mothers will make use of plastic coverings to protect vulnerable materials on the seats and bunks.

In the context of school, on the one hand it will be a novelty for some Traveller children to be able to move around inside a classroom and they will want to do this. On the other hand being expected to sit down for a considerable length of time without the opportunity to go outside will be unusual and difficult for some.

By the time they come into school Gypsy Traveller children will have listened to a good deal of adult conversation, which will have influenced their language, though they may have scant experience of books. They will have had the opportunity for much imaginative and imitative play outside, yet may not have been able to paint, cut, stick, thread beads, do puzzles or other activities which would help to develop their fine motor skills, as such activities would probably create too much mess inside even if there was room to engage in them. It is quite possible that a class teacher who was unfamiliar with the environment and culture that the children came from could initially make a distorted assessment of their abilities. A ten year old Traveller boy, coming into a new school, was asked by his teacher to do a drawing of a man as an initial assessment activity. She was shocked by his clumsiness with the pencil and later said to me that his picture scarcely matched what she would expect from a five year old and she wasn't sure where to begin with him. I suggested that she ask him to read to her, as I knew that his reading age almost matched his chronological age. She was duly amazed and impressed with his reading. I knew that the boy had been in and out of schools for short stays for years. He had a quick intelligence, was desperately keen to read and whenever he had the chance he practised, but he avoided writing whenever he could, as many children like him do, as he knew that his hands could not match what was in his head. This is not a situation peculiar to a Traveller child, but I mention it to demonstrate how accurate assessments can often be hard to make, especially for those whose education has been interrupted many times. It is important not to generalise about a group of children, who will each come into school with individual experiences, needs and abilities, but it is very easy to do.

There will be many interdependent factors that will affect both the achievement and behaviour of Traveller children coming into primary schools. Water is another one. The scarcity of water on many unofficial sites will certainly make the chance to play with water in school almost irresistible. Some children will be unfamiliar with taps and flush toilets and fascinated by the toilet and washing facilities available in school. Recently I took three primary aged children from a family stopping on the roadside into a new school and arranged to spend the morning there helping the children to settle in. The teachers made the girls very welcome, other children offered to be friends and in no time I was feeling happily redundant. I spent the morning listening to other children read and observing out of the corner of my eye the girls each sitting by a new friend, chattering and getting involved in what was going on. At lunchtime I left and said I would call in the next day to see if all was still going well. The following day I returned to hear of complete havoc at lunchtime as the girls had spent the entire time in the cloakrooms, washing, spraying others with water and having what must have been to them a most glorious water fight. They had it seemed been completely uncontrollable. For the next few days until the family was evicted, I had to spend every break time and lunchtime as an extra supervisor and water monitor.

In other families the necessary control and conservation of water at home with the attendant careful privacy for washing may well make a Traveller child shy and reluctant to change for PE in a mixed class, feelings which will probably be more intense in older children. The children have learnt that particular attention needs to be paid to the need for privacy when changing and washing in the context of their home lives with several people living in a confined space. It may therefore be difficult for some children to cope with the relaxed openness of a classroom.

At the primary stage it is likely to be the older children (say between seven and eleven-years-old) who will have the most difficulty in relating to one school after another. If they have had constantly interrupted school attendance they are not only likely to be academically behind their peer group, but also well aware of the fact.

Though they may have had unique experiences and have much knowledge in certain specialised areas, these will not be shared with others unless and until the children feel secure in their situation. The children will often adopt a variety of compensatory measures to disguise feelings of inadequacy – withdrawal, refusal, disruption – if they are not made comfortable in school. A Traveller child, who came into school after living for a year in a bender tent, was acutely sensitive to teasing about his lifestyle until a perceptive teacher gave credit to his knowledge in a class discussion about tent design. When other children asked what a 'bender' was, the teacher suggested that the child should make a drawing to put on the classroom wall and then asked other children to discuss the shapes of tents they had slept in. A whole lesson about shape and space, the use of materials, waterproofing and heating ensued in which the Traveller child was able to participate fully. He and his lifestyle were no longer the centre of attention, the focus of attention had shifted to aspects of science and design.

Children from highly mobile families may come into a new school after a series of emotional or even violent confrontations with the police or local residents and display quite agitated behaviour. What they will need most from their teachers is a sense of calm and reassurance. They will be helped by a knowledge that in the school and classroom at least no prejudice will be tolerated and that there is a stability and a structure to be followed. Yet some Traveller children, well used to attending school after school after school, handle the constant changes with a remarkable dignity and assurance. I spoke with a nun, head of a Roman Catholic primary school, a few days after a group of Irish Traveller children – cousins from two families – had come to her school. She was delighted with their behaviour and found it in marked contrast to many of the other children in the school, which served an estate with a high proportion of broken homes and single parent families. The Sister could sense the strong and caring family background that was giving a stability to these children, despite the constant moving on. One of the class teachers remarked on how refreshing it was to have children in her class who knew how to play in the home corner in her room once again. Her regular children no longer displayed that imaginative facility, she said.

There are many stories that can be told, but there are no generalisations. Traveller children may come into schools in any of the circumstances just detailed and others besides, showing some of the described attitudes, modes of behaviour or patterns of development. Unless the teachers they meet have some understanding of the range of cultural features and particular circumstances which Gypsy and other Traveller children bring with them to school, it will not be a comfortable place for them. The teachers who do offer the children space and time to adjust, who are patient in explaining the everyday school and classroom routines, who offer encouragement and appropriate differentiation in the work, who build on the skills the children already have and who adopt a flexible approach whilst demonstrating the standards of behaviour they would like, are the ones who enable the children to take what school can give them. Only in these conditions will the children flourish and develop, have equal opportunities in school and access to the curriculum.

From the first moment of contact parents (Travellers or not) have with a school they will have a sense of whether they, their culture and following this their children will be respected there. The tone of voice and the body language of the school administrator will convey its own message. The way the school admission form is presented for completion, the sensitivity or non-sensitivity to the possible illiteracy of the parents, will be keenly felt. The way the issue of school uniform is discussed will be significant. Insistence on full uniform for even known short-stay children has been used as a means to keep Traveller children out of school by those unwilling to take them. Allowing Traveller children to come into a fully uniformed school in other clothes without any consideration of the effects that this emphasis on difference will make to the children's ability to feel welcome and secure in class also demonstrates an insensitivity. Headteachers who discuss the uniform requirements of their schools with parents, possibly lend items of clothing, who make helpful suggestions about colours and styles that will be acceptable and blend in with what the other children are wearing, or who make it clear that whatever the children are wearing will make no difference at all to their acceptance by all in the school (and say this knowing that within the ethos of the school, this will be true) – these headteachers will be the ones who give parents confidence to let their children attend.

There are countless small indicators that parents will be sensitive to, particularly Gypsy Traveller parents, many of whom have grown up themselves surrounded by hostility and rejection.

> The morale of parents and carers of young children is undermined by discrimination and harassment and this too will affect the children themselves, however subtly. The issue is not just one of cultural exchange, important though that is in itself. True multicultural exchange cannot take place when one group is held in a consistently inferior position to the other. The issue is about relative power. (Reid 1992, p.17)

It could well be the case that outside the school gates angry confrontations are taking place about site issues. A group of Travellers may have arrived, as part of their working route, for a wedding, or to support sick relatives, in an area where there is no transit site and no legal place to stop. The spot they camped on during their previous visit has been blocked off or trenched to prevent re-entry. They will have pulled their trailers on to whatever space they can find and undoubtedly provoked an antagonistic reaction from residents living nearby. There will be calls for swift eviction and complaints to the police, who under the Criminal Justice Act of 1994 have powers to move families on within a very short time. Residents who are also parents of other children at the local school may express their resentment to the teaching staff. Teaching and non-teaching staff at the school may live nearby themselves and will certainly have their personal opinions, which have been coloured and determined by their own cultural upbringing and experiences.

If Traveller children are to feel secure and flourish in school, then whatever the hostility outside, school has to be a safe haven, a place where every member of staff both teaching and non-teaching is professional in attitude and exercise of judgement. Shortly after a small group of Traveller children had been enrolled at a new school the headteacher called me to her office. The family trailers were parked on the edge of an incomplete industrial estate a few hundred yards away. It was a stopping place which had not been used before and no Traveller children had attended this school previously. There had been no problem about places being available and the head had welcomed them into the school. The headteacher confessed though that she had been shocked suddenly to discover racism within her school, displayed in the comments and attitudes of several adult members of the school community. It was an all white school and following the 'No Problem Here' approach, no staff development sessions or in-service training had touched on these issues in the past. The equal opportunities policy, there in name, had to be brought sharply into practice.

The deep antagonism and resentment felt by many adults towards Gypsy and Traveller peoples simmers just below the surface and needs only a little provocation for it to break through. A group of families camped for several years on an unauthorised but tolerated site on the edge of a city and campaigned for a proper site to be built. The children attended the local primary school and as months turned to years they became happily settled there. Every few months some new development in the campaign for or against the site – a public meeting, a planning application, the formation of a residents' action group, an enquiry – would take place and be reported in the media. With depressing regularity in the following two or three days the Traveller children would come home from school upset and complaining of name-calling and victimisation in the playground. Plainly the media attention generated talk in all the local homes and the children came into school the next day trailing their parents' prejudices and comments with them. That these are not isolated instances is borne out by the OFSTED report:

> Some schools, which admitted to anxiety prior to the admission of Gypsy and New Traveller pupils, expressed surprise at the polite and calm dignity of the children and in retrospect had been more alarmed by the prejudiced attitudes and behaviour revealed by some of their non-Travelling pupils and parents. (OFSTED 1996, p.18, para.39)

Bullying by other children, name-calling, fear of what might happen in the playground are significant factors in both the willingness of Traveller children to go to school and the preparedness of parents to put them there.

> As a consequence of their own negative school experiences, parents are often fearful of their children leaving the home community. They may be apprehensive about the safety of their children in school. Will they escape from the playground? Will they be ostracised? Will they be the target of racial abuse? Will they be considered unintelligent through gaps in their schooling? Will they lose their cultural identity? The one question that encompasses all these issues is, most importantly, will they be happy? (Fraser and Wood 1991, p.44)

Following a highly publicised incident when a child was taken by a stranger from a school playground, Traveller parents were extremely anxious about the possibility of their own children being abducted from school, and for a while many children were kept at home, despite the fact that the original incident had taken place in another part of the country far away from the one in which they were living. The children themselves are more likely to worry about what is going on in the playground. For many young children the notion of 'going out to play' is confusing in itself when they have been thinking that all the activities they have been engaged in in the classroom throughout the morning have been 'play'. To be sent outside to a space devoid of objects to play with, full of children who may tease and taunt, is anything but play. The arrival of any group of new children will unsettle the existing peer relationships in the classroom and playground. When the new group are Traveller children I have often seen how the forming of relationships will be given extra dimensions of preconceptions and stereotyping among both Travellers and non-Travellers The potential for confrontation and bullying will be higher. It is difficult for Traveller children to come to schools simply as themselves, without having to cope with the image and experience of their group.

Within the classroom the teacher's approach is vital in every area: 'Teacher expectations of children are crucial to their achievements so it needs saying that teachers must look at themselves and their own attitudes to the ways of life of others' (Stevenson 1992, p.35).

It is obvious that a personally prejudiced attitude on the part of the teacher will adversely affect their working relationship with Traveller children, but the most concerned and sympathetic teacher can still exclude the group by their choice of the range of resources that are available in the classroom and the contexts in which the curriculum is delivered. In the last fifteen years there has been an explosion in the number and variety of resources available to schools which deal with Gypsy and Traveller cultures in one way or another. There are books, photographs, pictures, puzzles, videos, craft artifacts, resource packs, games, worksheets, the list could go on. Yet often these resources are produced locally and on a small scale by Traveller Education Services (of which more will be told in the next chapter) and only get into schools where Traveller children are already enrolled. It has to be positive and affirming for Traveller children, as all others, to be able to work with materials in which the context is understandable and relevant to them and in which they can recognise their own cultures, but not helpful if they are the only children in the class working with such materials or if the materials arrive with or hard on the heels of the children themselves. This will only serve to accentuate 'otherness' at a time when integration is sought and tend to confirm the exotic stereotype or a deficit model in which 'special' materials are needed to help these children. If resources based in Gypsy and Traveller cultures are already in current use in classrooms when the children arrive and are familiar to the teacher and the other children they will feel themselves at ease. Many times I have witnessed a child's excitement when they discovered a story which reflected their own lives on the shelves in the classroom. One child, formerly shy and reticent, was so pleased to find a story about Appleby Fair in the class library that he brought a family video, of their own latest visit to Appleby to sell horses, in to share with the class.

At the moment few schools without Traveller children on roll now or in the past have many such resources. Teachers will only obtain them and use them if they know about them in the first place and then only if they are convinced that they will be appropriate and useful in the delivery of the national curriculum for all children. There are in fact many opportunities for positive perspectives of Gypsy and of other Traveller groups to be included by teachers in their schemes of work for all children throughout the curriculum. Increasingly there are books which could bring Traveller cultures into the classroom if studied as texts during the Literacy Hour. Some of these are catalogued in *Beyond the Stereotype* (Devon Traveller Education Service 1995), a booklet in which ideas and resource lists are given for such perspectives and contexts in both topic-based and subject-based formats. I knew from my own experience for instance how careful Travelling families have to be with the use of water and how much they contribute to the recycling of metals. All this can easily be included in work on conservation and the environment. The invention of steam powered roundabouts and the new wonder of electric light, seen by many in rural areas for the first time at the fairs brought in by the Showmen, offer interesting contexts for all children studying the Industrial Revolution and Victorian times. The Gypsy Traveller artist/craftsmen who built and decorated the wooden, horse-drawn wagons could easily be studied within the art curriculum. There are many examples that could be given. If Traveller children come into school, recognise a respect for themselves displayed in the materials around them and are not treated as 'extra-ordinary', they will be confident to speak for themselves and they will be able to identify themselves without shame or fear. Then they will be able to realise their potential.

The OFSTED report again makes the point simply and clearly:

> Travelling pupils appear to achieve higher standards in schools which place great emphasis on equality of opportunity and by encouraging the acceptance of cultural and ethnic diversity, establish an ethos which fosters self-esteem and pride in individual and group identity.
> (OFSTED 1996, p.18, para. 38)

For some Travelling groups there is no possibility of hiding their identity and celebrating their culture can be overdone. I expect most teachers of Travellers have heard the frustration and resignation in the tones of voice from children travelling with circuses when they report that they have been expected to give yet another talk about their way of life to their new classmates of that particular week. One child from a circus family told me that now every time he goes into a new school he brings the topic up with the class teacher as soon as he can. He knows that at some stage during his stay he will be asked to give the talk, so now he offers to do this straightaway at the beginning of the week so that he can 'get it over with' and then join in with the work of the class. Using children as a resource in this way is undoubtedly interesting for the other children, probably makes the teacher feel that they are celebrating and accepting the culture brought into school, but it does little to allow the circus children to develop themselves. Contrast this with the experience given by one school to a group of Russian children travelling in England with a circus in 1996. At three days notice the school was asked to take in the six children of varying ages for a week. After discussion with one of the parents who acted as spokesperson for the rest and with members of the school staff it was decided that, whilst everyone thought the children should experience the full range of the curriculum, the most positive contribution to the children's education that could be made in the short time available would be to improve their spoken English. Therefore the children each shadowed another child, who volunteered to be a friend and mentor through the week as they attended the regular classes. The fact that the circus was in town could not be denied, but those teachers who wanted to include this resource in their work took groups of children out of school and to the circus where they talked to adults from that community who were pleased with the public relations exercise.

A teenage girl from the Showmen's community, begged me to tell her school to stop giving her books to read about the fairground. 'I know about the fair', she said, 'I live it every day. I'm interested in all the things that other teenagers are. Why can't they give me books like they give them to everyone else?'

For some Gypsy Traveller families, however, those who are in housing or relatively settled or who live at a distance from their school, it is possible for their children not to be readily identified as Travellers. Some schools believe this is the best way to proceed, though the OFSTED report suggests otherwise:

> where the ethos of the school implicitly or explicitly suggests that Travelling pupils are best served by an incognito status, and this is particularly so for Gypsies and New Travellers, the response (to school of Traveller pupils) lacks confidence, is tentative and reserved. (OFSTED 1996, p.18, para.38)

Case studies from the South West region also demonstrate how damaging it can be for schools to hide the identity of pupils in the presumed interests of 'treating everybody the same'.

> RC left school suddenly after a letter was sent home accusing her of smoking on the school bus: she was not. The Deputy who sent the letter was unaware that she was a Gypsy Traveller and that her parents could not read. The letter was read to the father by a relative and he was highly embarrassed. He was so angry with the school that he removed his daughter and threatened to leave the area taking his four sons out of primary school as well. (South West Region Traveller Conference 1996)

and:

> CC left after an incident in a classroom when the teacher was unaware of her background. A discussion took place about people being more unfortunate than those in class. Homosexuals, tramps and 'Gyppos' were listed. CC revealed her background and said what she thought

about the class. She did not return to school the next day and 'has gone
up country'. (ibid. 1996)

If a headteacher believes that prejudiced attitudes will be the result of the
identification of a child as a Gypsy Traveller, then it is more important for them
to work on the racism in the school than to attempt to hide the fact that the child
is there. It is a poor protection for a child to be obliged to deny themselves.

Some Traveller parents will bring their children into school identifying
themselves and their children with pride, as a matter of course. Others will have
another motive in self-identification. Recently a headteacher told me of a
mother who brought her three children to his primary school for a week whilst
they attended a family wedding some miles away. She was most concerned that
he understood that they were Gypsies, and in no way to be associated with 'New
Age Travellers' and all the negative stereotyping that she believed would
accompany such a connection. There is an awareness of shifts in public opinion
in relation to them, which Gypsy Traveller people engage with at all times. This
constantly affects their dealings with other groups.

Other Traveller parents, bringing their children to primary schools,
explicitly ask the headteachers not to identify their children as Gypsies or
Travellers. Their anxieties are presumably such that they feel their children will
only suffer or face discrimination if identified. They fear that their culture will
only be degraded, not respected, in the school. The children are instructed to
keep their home lives to themselves and to evade questioning. Children can
become extremely adept at such passing, but can only be diminished by it, and
probably confused too.

It is an extremely sensitive area of concern and one which will have to be
confronted as plans for monitoring of achievement by ethnic group including
Gypsy Travellers are developed by the Department for Education and
Employment (DfEE) in the near future. There are also plans to issue unique pupil
identifying numbers to enable the tracing of the developing achievement of
pupils and the facilitation of the exchange of educational records between
schools. If any lack of educational achievement by a particular ethnic group of
pupils is to be identified and measures introduced to improve their chances of
academic success, then monitoring by ethnic identity is essential. However, it is
easy to appreciate the concern of some parents about ethnic identification when
levels of antagonism and prejudice remain high. It is crucial that there can be
trust between teachers and Traveller parents.

Only such a trust will allow the children to relax and be able to grow in an
atmosphere where they feel supported by parents and school alike. Both parents
and teachers need to understand and appreciate the others' agenda. A report
from a Save the Children project in the north of England picked up the lack of
this vital connection: 'I often feel that it must be difficult for a Traveller child to
keep the interest for school going as there is little or no positive reinforcement
for his/her achievements at home' (Arnold et al. 1992, p.20).

If parents cannot or do not support what the school is doing, if teachers fail to understand parents' anxieties and fears, the children cannot be at ease between the two. Take sex education as an example. Many primary schools will incorporate elements of sex education naturally into the curriculum within topics of life-cycles, growth and living things. Their policy for this will have been discussed and approved by the governors and be outlined in the school prospectus. A non-literate Gypsy Traveller parent placing a child in a school for a few weeks whilst travelling is unlikely to make themselves familiar with the details of the school's policies and may be distressed when their children come home one day and talk of some of the things they have been discussing in class. Some Gypsy Traveller parents do not approve of the open discussion of sex in any circumstances. Others, who will not talk to children on these matters themselves, are willing for schools to take on sex education if it has been agreed with parents first. Others again would be unhappy at such discussions within a mixed group. Some teachers will not understand or have patience with these attitudes or have time to communicate with parents individually. It is easy for misunderstandings and confrontations to arise, that leave the children embarrassed and muddled, or may even result in them being removed from the school.

Traveller children need their parents and teachers to work in partnership if they are to settle and succeed in primary school, growing through a broad curriculum. Yet this leads to another area of debate, for the teacher will see the curriculum as far broader than just reading and writing – a developing of the potential of the whole child. 'The needs of the young Traveller child are not simply to read and write and retain a sense of culture, but to continue that culture into future generations from a position of greater strength' (Duncan 1992, p.58).

Gypsy Traveller parents may feel that the very broadening, the strengthening of the individual potential, the opening of choice will threaten the whole basis of their family based culture. The Traveller child in school poses another set of questions concerning who or what they are being educated for.

CHAPTER THREE

Questions of Access

Before a more detailed look at the purposes of education for Traveller children, there is a need to go back a little, as the fundamental question of access is still not fully resolved.

This chapter seeks to clarify the position of access to school in England for Travelling children today by looking at the several factors which affect it. A wider European perspective will follow in a later chapter. The developments in educational practice and policy affecting Travellers over the last twenty years will not be recounted or surveyed as this has been ably done from the beginning of the twentieth century by Derek Hawes and Barbara Perez (Hawes and Perez 1995) and from the 1970s more recently by Mary Waterson (Waterson 1997). The emphasis here is on a consideration of the present situation and the reality of access to mainstream schools for Gypsy and Traveller children.

Legally all children have the same rights of access to school. The 1944 Education Act confirmed and enshrined the rights of every child to a full-time education, laying duties on LEAs to ensure that sufficient school places were available and on parents to ensure that their children either attended school or received an adequate and suitable education in some other way. Parents must ensure that their children receive: 'an efficient full time education suitable to his age, ability and aptitude and to any special educational needs he may have by regular attendance at school or otherwise' (DES 1944).

Despite this, through the 1970s there were still instances of Gypsy Traveller children being denied school places because their families were camped illegally. The issue was brought to a head by the case of Mary Delaney who in 1977 was refused admission to a school in Croydon by the local authority as she came from an unauthorised site. Both ACERT and the then National Gypsy Education Council (NGEC) mounted strong protests at this denial of a basic right and threatened to take action in the European Court. The pressure met with success in that the 1980 Education Act and the DES Circular 1/81 made it quite clear that an authority's duties to make school places available extended to every child: 'The reference to children "in the area" of the authority means that each authority's duty extends to all children residing in their area, whether permanently or temporarily. The duty thus embraces in particular travelling children, including Gypsies' (DES 1981, Clause 5).

No authority would deny the legal right of a travelling child to a school place today and the majority of headteachers run schools with an inclusive ethos. However the recent introduction and publication of league tables of schools' performance indicators has undoubtedly lead to extra pressures on headteachers and a wariness in some cases about accepting pupils who it is supposed might contribute to a drop in the school's performance in terms of achievement or attendance. Discussions within the day conferences of the National Association of Teachers of Travellers (NATT), which was founded in 1980, have revealed instances of subtle and not so subtle discrimination. Headteachers for example might be quite specific that places were only available in certain year groups, knowing full well the reluctance of Traveller families to split their children up or might be most particular in their absolute insistence on the wearing of correct uniform, despite the difficulties they are aware this inevitably causes for mobile families. Other schools have operated unreasonably lengthy admissions procedures which have effectively denied places to short-stay families. Such obstacles placed in the way of access amount to a culture of discrimination and exclusion in those schools which create these difficulties unnecessarily.

Schools which do accept Traveller pupils on to their rolls may also, however, be quick to exclude. One of the main findings of the OFSTED report on education for Travelling children was that: 'A disproportionate number of Travelling pupils, particularly at the secondary phase, are excluded from school. This is despite the general assessment that the behaviour of Travelling pupils is good' (OFSTED 1996, p.8).

A readiness to exclude can often be related to anxieties about overall school performances. There are also many instances of unwelcoming attitudes in schools leading either to pupils deciding to exclude themselves or to their parents removing them or condoning non-attendance.

There is a certain leeway allowed in the legal attendance requirements for children from travelling families. The legal minimum attendance, confirmed in section 199(6) of the 1993 Education Act (DfE 1993), is for 200 sessions (100 days) over a period of twelve months. It is made quite clear in guidance from the Department for Education and Employment (DfEE 1994) that the spirit of this legislation is to protect families from unreasonable prosecution when their need to travel for work may make full-time schooling impossible. It is in no way intended as a denial of equal entitlement to access or an acceptance that part-time education is sufficient. On the contrary, the guidance encourages as much school attendance as is possible:

> It does not mean that part-time education for Travelling children is legally acceptable, nor does it relieve parents of their duties under section 36 of the 1944 Education Act, to ensure that children are receiving suitable education when not at school. (OFSTED 1996, p.20, para. 43)

The DfEE has also made it clear (DfEE 1994) that unavoidable temporary absences from school due to parents having to travel periodically for work may be classed as authorised absences and should not affect the schools' attendance figures pejoratively. Schools have been encouraged by teachers in Traveller Education Services, who work closely with Traveller families, to keep those Traveller children on roll, who it is known are travelling seasonally for work. Where it is known that the children will be returning regularly to the same school, which becomes known as their 'base' school, their absence can be recorded as 'authorised' as the legislation allows. This is done so that the school places will be reserved for the children to take up on their return. It is a significant factor in the new marketplace for school places which has rendered some popular schools oversubscribed with every place falling vacant quickly filled. However, difficulties occurred when Travelling children were temporarily enrolled for brief periods (quite possibly without the knowledge of their base schools) at other schools whilst their families were working away because dual enrolment was not allowed in law. Either the child had to come off the roll of their regular base school and risk losing their place, or they could not access other schools as they travelled. Either way the possibility of a reasonable continuity of education was being diminished. Those involved in supporting the education of Travelling children know how important the factor of a continuing and trusting relationship with a regular school is in determining the success of a child's time there. Support teachers did not wish the Traveller children to be removed from the roll of their base schools if subsequent temporary enrolments became known which would mean the permanent loss of the places in the base schools. It was a difficult situation and there were uncertainties about the best procedure to follow. There were a number of discussions with officials in the DfEE and finally in January 1998 amendments were made to the law to allow dual registration at schools for Traveller children in these circumstances.

It can be seen from all of the above that whilst there is a clear legal entitlement, the access to school for Travelling children is still not always straightforward.

Whatever the legal rights of access for Travelling children it became quite clear, after the highlighting of the attendance of the group at less than 10 per cent in the Plowden report (DES 1967), through the 1970s and 1980s that an 'Open Door' policy was not sufficient. Chris Reiss' Schools Council study (Reiss 1975) made a very rough estimate that between 10 per cent and 25 per cent of Gypsy Traveller children were sometimes enrolled at school (statistics for 1969 and 1970) but this did not in any way mean regular attendance. Eight years later the HMI discussion paper (DES 1983) that suggested that only 40 per cent to 50 per cent of primary aged children from Travelling families were attending school for even part of the year. At that time as few as 10 per cent to 15 per cent of secondary aged pupils were thought to be registered at school. In 1996, when OFSTED produced its next report, it stated that: 'Although the number of Travelling children registered with schools has increased substantially in the last 10 years, there is still a marked contrast between the total number of Travelling pupil registrations and those attending on a regular basis' (OFSTED 1996, p.19, para. 42). And at the secondary stage thousands of young Travellers are still avoiding or being denied access to school altogether: 'Access to the curriculum for secondary aged children remains a matter of grave concern. There are possibly as many as 10,000 (Traveller) children at this phase who are not even registered with a school' (OFSTED 1996, p.8).

In the substantial increase, at least in enrolment at primary schools in the last ten years, the development of Traveller Education Services (TES) across the country has undoubtedly played a significant part. The DES knew from the evidence of its inspectorate that some positive action was necessary if enrolments were to increase. From the early 1970s some pioneering authorities had begun to develop services which aimed to make contact with Traveller families and support their take up of educational opportunities. In those early days a good deal of outreach and on-site work was done and several mobile teaching units were deployed. The motives for using the mobile units varied from one authority to another. Some were considered necessary bridges to school, when it was felt that a period of assessment, development of families' understandings of what school work involved and basic skills teaching on site were important preparations for an eventual successful move into mainstream school. At other times and in other places mobile classrooms were felt to be a realistic, rapid response to the needs of short-stay families either working through an area or being evicted swiftly from it. Others again provided a segregated education in situations where intense local hostility, in turn provoking great anxiety in Traveller parents, forestalled any attempts to place the children in local schools (Hawes and Perez 1995).

The debate over the use of mobile teaching units raised and sometimes clouded the issue of integration and assimilation. Many teachers were working towards complete integration of Traveller children in mainstream schools as soon as possible as an issue of rights and entitlement for the children, and were wholly against the use of mobile teaching units. Other teachers felt that some access to formal education was better than none and that on-site teaching was perhaps a necessary stage on the way to successful integration in school. Many parents feared that assimilation rather than integration, a denial of culture, would be the result of school attendance. If they could have teachers coming to them at home providing access to basic literacy, that was all they wanted from state education. There were many tensions as teachers and parents struggled to reach an understanding.

Education Welfare Officers (EWOs) could find themselves in difficult situations where they had to make professional judgements with great sensitivity if they were to be successful in establishing regular school attendance by Gypsy Traveller children. A heavy handed or confrontational approach insisting on attendance at secondary school by an older child in a family, with the threat of court action as a sanction, could lead to the family moving away from an area, taking younger siblings out of primary schools as an unintended and destructive consequence.

Over a period of years a number of specialist EWOs, who would seek to balance legal and cultural considerations, were appointed to Traveller Education Services. The experience of support teachers grew and relationships between teachers, schools and families developed. As the political implications of anything that suggested a segregated education were worked through, more and more children were admitted directly to school and the use of the mobile units as a preparation for school declined. They began to be used more for pre-school projects and as resource spaces for peripatetic teachers supporting distance learning providing educational continuity between schools.

A decisive factor in the development of the Traveller Education Services was the confirmation by the DES during the 1980s that 'no area pool' money could legitimately be used to fund them. Every local authority was obliged to pay into the centrally held 'no area pool' each year and then claim back from this budget such expenses as were incurred beyond the ordinary when meeting the needs of children who were not permanently resident in the authority. Thus salaries for peripatetic and support teachers and costs for transport or mobile classrooms used to respond to the perceived needs of Traveller children could be reclaimed. In fact as every LEA had to contribute to the 'no area pool' anyway, it was in their best interests to claim as much money back from that budget as possible. This took the issue away from the local political debate, where it was quite clear from the extreme negative reactions to any plans for site building, following the 1968 Caravan Sites Act, that there would be public hostility to any priority being given to develop educational provision for Travelling children within the local authority budget.

In my own authority, when a possible location for a site was given publicity in the press, there was an immediate letter of concern from the headteacher of the local primary school stating that existing parents were extremely worried that Gypsy Traveller children might attend the school. On another occasion a councillor wrote an angry letter to the local paper complaining about an advertisement for a peripatetic support teacher for the Traveller Education Service, declaring that there were surely many higher priorities than such a post. A documentary from the BBC's Community Programme Unit about site provision in the 1980s showed a demonstration by parents with placards – 'KEEP YOUR CHILDREN OUT OF SCHOOL IF GYPSIES MOVE IN'.

Without central government making it clear that they understood the need for positive action if Gypsy Traveller children were to have greater access to school and any chance of an equal educational opportunity, and that they were willing for no area pool money to be used to support this, much of the progress that has been made would not have been possible. Central government commitment was essential for any substantial development to take place at the local level. This remains equally true today. There are constant reminders of neighbourhood prejudice as in Gloucestershire early in 1998 when a large group of parents took their children out of school when Gypsy Traveller children were given temporary places there.

In 1990 the funding system for Traveller Education Services was changed. From this point on authorities were invited to bid for funding for Traveller Education projects, most commonly for three years at a time under section 210 (now section 488) of the Education Act in competition with all other LEAs. All bids for projects would need to 'be aimed at ensuring unhindered access to, and full integration in mainstream education' (DES 1990). The DES would pay grants of 75 per cent to successful bids. No longer would there be the notionally infinite resource of the 'no area pool'. From the inception of the section 210 grants to the present time the government education department (now the Department for Education and Employment, DfEE) has been managing the limited overall budget available (approx. £11,000,000 in 1998) and its contribution to it (reduced to 65 per cent in 1995), to try to achieve a more even pattern of provision across the country. When the specific grants were introduced in 1990 it was anticipated that the level of grant available would meet the needs which had been expressed through claims on the no area pool. However, in the event several authorities which had not been claiming or only partly claiming from 'the pool' decided that this was the appropriate moment to develop their Traveller education provision and the available budget did not cover all the bids received. Therefore initially only existing projects were funded, and in later bidding rounds larger services had their budgets cut in order to allow other authorities to start services. Latterly nearly every service has had some reduction in funding to enable the existing budget to be spread more widely, if more thinly. In 1997 some 82 LEAs, some in consortia, out of 109 provided a service funded largely from what is now called section 488 grant. Local Government Reorganisation is currently changing and increasing the numbers of local authorities and a new bidding round is due to take place in autumn 1998 for specific grants for Traveller Education projects to take effect from April 1999. It is vital to the continuing access to school for Traveller children that the present government affirms its commitment to social inclusion by making a sufficient budget available, which will enable authorities to meet the assessed needs of Traveller children.

The size and nature of Traveller Education Services vary enormously depending on length of establishment, geographical location, numbers of Travellers, travelling patterns of families, degree of settlement, site availability and so on, and the roles played by TES staff are many. They work inside schools and often visit homes, offering teaching and other support to children, schools and families. They perform extensive liaison roles both between schools and families and various other agencies (health, social services, etc.). They promote access to pre-school, adult basic education and other community education provision and offer in-service training to teachers. The staff (often including specialist Education Welfare Officers) develop policies and systems in many fields from arranging transport, easing transfer to secondary education and promoting attendance, to managing structures for distance learning. Culturally based and other materials are collected and developed in various media and disseminated by the peripatetic teams of teachers and through resource centres. The educational resources developed are of many kinds. They may be standard curriculum materials specially adapted for distance learning. Culturally specific materials will be produced not only for the use of Traveller children in school, but for use by all children to increase their awareness of these minority groups. This list of the tasks which TES teams perform is not exhaustive, but I suspect that agreement would be almost universal to the proposition that much of the work undertaken before the children even start at school – the outreach work, the visits, the communication and the development of trusting relationships between Traveller families and those within the formal education system – has been and remains crucial.

From all around the country the same message comes through.

From Essex:

> The role of the Traveller Teacher ... has become a key feature in the successes that we have experienced, because of the length of time in post the teacher has become well known to Traveller families in the area who often will say that they trust the school and that it understands and accommodates Traveller pupils. (Blaney 1996, p.30)

From Cardiff:

> Successful secondary schooling for Travellers must be based on a consenting, participating partnership between home and school. (Clay 1996, p.38)

From Surrey:

> I worked hard as 'go-between' building trusting, working relationships between the parents and school, explaining letters, assessment procedures, the importance of parent consultations, their role in the successful education of their children, and the place of school trips in their learning and experience. With time and effort on the part of the school, the family and myself, attitudes on both sides began to change. (Evans 1996, p.40)

From Lancashire:

> The Lancashire TES ... Education Welfare Officers ... work closely with Traveller families whilst they are resident in the county. They deal not only with attendance and school issues but spend time getting to know the families and building up a degree of trust. It is recognised

that parental support is crucial if we are to make any headway in improving school enrolments and attendance. (Kenyon 1996, p.46)

From Wiltshire:

I feel we have built up a trust between us and this has moved the situation on tremendously. (Worth 1996, p.73)

From Cambridgeshire:

Much of the home-school work of Traveller education teams is designed to pave the way for improved dialogue between the various parties involved. In many instances, section 210 teachers and home-school liaison officers act as intermediaries, attempting to develop trusting relationships and to raise awareness in the hope that, eventually, direct lines of communication will be established. (Wood 1997, p.75)

From the West Midlands and Scotland:

Schools with proactive home-school policies and practice, or schools which work closely with TESS, endeavour to use outreach strategies to meet parents in the security of their own environment. They work to build a shared understanding of parent and school expectations because the interests of the child is at the heart of the liaison process. (Holmes and Jordan 1997, p.96)

Without the sensitive, proactive and remarkably committed work of the staff of mainstream schools and the Traveller Education Services many Traveller children would never get as far as the school door.

Unfortunately whilst central and local education departments have been acting positively to encourage and enable Traveller children to take up their legal entitlement to mainstream educational opportunities, the policies of other government departments have undermined the possibilities of access for some. The issues of accommodation and access to education (and healthcare) have always been closely interlinked. Without a place to stop obviously school attendance is impossible. For families under threat of eviction, having no more than a few days or a week or two on a ground, the daily business of survival, earning a living, getting water and shopping, finding a wash house for laundry, looking for another place to move to, will inevitably often have to have a higher priority than finding a school for the children. There is much credit to be given to the determination of families and the openness and flexibility of schools that many children are put in schools for just a few days at a time as their parents are forced from place to place.

Every few months I receive a telephone call from Mrs. M. to tell me that she and her family are back in the area again. They have no regular base, but travel widely for work throughout the UK and sometimes over in Germany. She says where she is stopping – always a new spot as the place where they stayed the last time will inevitably have been blocked off, trenched or made inaccessible in some other way – and asks if her children can go back into the school they attended on their previous visit. We check with the school, discuss the numbers, the distance and the transport implications and visit the family. Mrs. M. knows she wants the same school as before because her children were made welcome and were happy there, so she may drive the children in herself or move, if she can, to a camping place nearer to the school. For its part the school also knows how much easier it will be for the children to return to a familiar environment and they find the temporary places somehow, lend school uniform sweatshirts and look out the folders of the children's work that they have kept from the time they were there before. For a week or two the children are back in the school. The class teacher contacts the previous school, noted on the green record exchange card which Mrs. M. keeps, for records or a progress report. Then, as they are camping illegally, they are moved on.

When another family with a similar travelling pattern arrived in our county once more last year, I would have expected the same procedure. However, this time Mrs. C. said that whilst her three younger ones would be going into school, Johnny, her eldest aged ten, would not be going this time. He was refusing to go. I went to find Johnny who was trying to keep well out of the way and asked him what the trouble was. He answered me with an uncharacteristic seriousness: 'Well, I've had some bad experiences at school since I last saw you, Miss. We've been shifted that much I'm not going any more'. During the next few days I talked more with Johnny and we planned a school visit, but before it could take place, the family was evicted from the car park where they were stopping illegally.

As I described in the first chapter of this book, many people had hoped that the duties laid on authorities in part two of the Caravan Sites Act 1968 to provide sites for Gypsies would lead to sufficient accommodation being provided within a reasonable time. However whilst authorities, who did build sites and make at least the minimum provision of fifteen pitches, were quick to apply for 'designation', a status which then entitled them to evict any Travellers not on a site from the borough, overall site provision was slow. Tom Lee, speaking for the Romany Guild, wrote in a pamphlet published in 1973:

> During the last 4 months, 15 applications have been made by local authorities for designation orders from the D of E plus 3 for exemption.... So far 14 boroughs have already been designated including Plymouth, Wolverhampton, Manchester and areas in East London. If only half of the applications before the Department of the Environment are granted designation status this will mean that several hundred Traveller families will be evicted and expelled from the areas where most of them have spent their lives. (Lee 1973, p.1)

Three years after that pamphlet, during the time I spent working for ACERT in London I assisted Tom Lee in producing a second booklet and found there had been little improvement.

> Three years later the situation of the Travellers has scarcely changed. Indeed with every new designation order it becomes worse, with Gypsies being virtually outlawed from boroughs which have been their homes for generations.... At 31st December 1975, throughout the whole of the country 1,459 pitches had been provided on 92 permanent sites and 526 pitches had been provided on 35 temporary sites.... Obviously a totally inadequate number and this in eight years.
> (Lee 1976, pp.1 and 4)

It meant that as a rough estimate about half of the families travelling had nowhere legal to park their trailers.

Another Gypsy Traveller writing in the same pamphlet expressed the anger and frustration felt by many: 'I still have to steal water and find the nearest public toilets. I still have to steer clear of 'no go' areas, be refused a drink in some pubs, watch my children and grand-children grow up uneducated' (Cooper 1976, p.15).

The Department of the Environment was also well aware that the Act was not having the effect of swift site building as had been anticipated and desired and Sir John Cripps was invited to compile a report on the working of the 1968 Act (Cripps 1977). He agreed that site provision had been unacceptably slow and highlighted the intense local hostility to any site plan put forward by an authority as a major factor. His recommendation that 100 per cent grants should be made available from central government for site building, to take at least the financial issue out of the local political debate was accepted and put into effect. Also it was recommended that in areas where Gypsies were buying their own land and seeking planning permission to live on it, some particular consideration should be given by planning committees to the fact the Gypsies had extraordinary difficulties in securing legal accommodation. This was due both to the insufficient number of official sites and to the fact that even if families desired to go into council housing they often faced hostility and prejudice on estates too.

Yet the depth of public antagonism to new sites, the fact that no time scale was put on to the providing of sites and the unwillingness of government to enforce the act strictly meant that site building continued to be slow. Complications were arising from the definition of 'Gypsy' which for the purposes of the Act was given as 'persons of nomadic habit of life whatever their race or origin'. During the 1970s and 1980s many young people were moving out from housing to live on the road, driven or choosing to go for a multitude of different personal, economic and social reasons. Increasingly through the courts the 'New' Travellers were claiming Gypsy status and site provision under the terms of the 1968 Act.

The situation was unsatisfactory from everyone's point of view, though for very different reasons. Central government, under the premiership of Margaret Thatcher, did not look kindly on those who were demonstrating so publicly an alienation from the society in which they had been raised. Local authorities did not wish to be obliged to provide more sites to include other groups of Travellers, whom they did not believe were covered by the original intention of the Act, despite fitting into the definition of 'Gypsy' which had been adopted. Many Gypsy Travellers resented the fact that some of the New Travellers, more familiar with legal procedures than they, might win court cases and achieve site provision before they themselves did – a kind of queue jumping. This was coupled with a resentment that the extreme negative stereotype of New Travellers created by intense media coverage of large gatherings in the mid 1980s had made life on the road more difficult for all. In their turn those New Travellers, who were trying to pursue nomadic lifestyles, saw no reason why they should face discrimination in site provision when the conditions and prejudice they endured were no different from those of other Traveller groups who were obliged to camp illegally due to a shortfall of official places to stop.

Rather than insisting on the full implementation of the 1968 Caravan Sites Act, providing a countrywide network of sites and assistance with planning permission for those who could afford to buy their own plots of land, the government took the decision to repeal it as part of the Criminal Justice and Public Order Act (CJA), 1994. Thus the duty of local authorities to provide sites was removed altogether. This decision was taken despite the fact that the overwhelming response to consultations was against it and despite a vote in the House of Lords which had recommended delaying this repeal for five years. At the same time any help which might have been given to Gypsy Travellers in the planning process for those seeking to make their own private sites was removed – to make it a level playing field for all.

Today, with no obligation any more on authorities to provide sites, it is estimated that the shortfall in site provision adversely affects approximately a third of Gypsy Traveller families at any one time (OFSTED 1996), and the penalties for illegal camping brought in by the CJA are harsher. Families with no place to stop can now be criminalised. After complaint, families may be directed to move from land immediately, even where the owner of the land is not known, and told not to return within three months. Refusal to comply with an order to move may result in arrest, fine, imprisonment and the confiscation of the vehicle. The powers given to the police by the CJA are such that often simply the threat of its use is sufficient to move a group of families on. The CJA demonstrated a clear will to force people off the road into settled accommodation denying the right to a nomadic habit of life enshrined in the 1968 Act, though it is hard to reconcile this with the fact that approximately 90 per cent of private planning applications by Gypsy Travellers meet with initial refusal.

For the families with no legal place to be the options are few and bleak. Trying to get a school based education with any kind of continuity for children in these circumstances is difficult indeed. For some, who experience a series of swift evictions right across the country there is scant chance for school access at all.

The 1994 Criminal Justice and Public Order Act is only the latest piece of legislation which has been oppressive to Gypsy Traveller families, who have been subject to persecution and harassment for most of the five hundred or so years since they first set foot in this country (Fraser 1992). Most contacts with officialdom have been confrontational and most state institutions associated with pressure to conform to a sedentary norm. In these circumstances it is interesting to consider the increased motivation of Gypsy Traveller parents over the last twenty years to place their children in schools at least at the primary phase, and to speculate on the reasons that have brought about the 'convergence' identified by Liégeois (see Chapter 1) as educationalists have reached out to them.

To survive as an independent ethnic group within a society that has been overwhelmingly hostile to them, Gypsy Travellers have adopted several strategies. They have preserved and value above all a strong extended family structure which offers a network of support to all within it, young and old alike. Within this kinship bond the children are reared, to look after each other, to learn to make a living, to take on their roles of responsibility within the group. They care for younger siblings from an early age, take part in earning the family living by working alongside their parents as soon as they are old enough, learn of their history and heritage from their grand parents.

Movement has also been a strong element in survival – movement for work opportunities to survive economically, movement away from trouble or hostility, travel to be with other family members in times of celebration or mourning, travel to fairs and markets to maintain friendships and work opportunities within the wider group.

Others have given up the nomadic habit (though always with the possibility of resuming it) moving into housing or on to permanent sites to avoid the stresses of the road for a while. These decisions though have often generated new stresses as neighbours have not always been welcoming and the extended family is not necessarily close at hand to give support. Settlement has denied the possibility of following work opportunities in the old ways and if new ways of earning a living have proved difficult to find there has been an attendant loss of independence and self-esteem.

Conditions on many of the council run sites have contributed to this loss of independence. Regulations on some only permit short periods away, after which entitlements to the pitch have to be relinquished. So it becomes more difficult to travel seasonally for work. The shortage in the number of site places overall means that there can be no guarantee that another one will be available on a family's return. Very few sites provide working areas within their boundaries for such activities as collecting and sorting scrap metal and so work opportunities from a settled base are curtailed. The limitation of self employed work possibilities has not been counterbalanced by an equivalent increase in waged job opportunities for those settled Travellers who would take these up, as much discrimination occurs and for some, a lack of literacy inevitably reduces chances of employment. Therefore in many cases on settled sites adult Travellers will come to depend on state benefits and resent and exploit the system which erodes their pride in their identity.

Whilst some families have found themselves in a downward spiral, others have recognised the inevitability of continuing change within their culture as in the cultures of all communities and have responded to it positively. It has been an adaptability, a resourcefulness and an ability to see opportunities within new circumstances that have in themselves been strong factors in the survival of the Gypsy Travellers as a distinct group. Some parents have seen that though their own education might have been entirely within the family and it has been possible to manage and often succeed well in financial terms without literacy, this is increasingly difficult. Many of the traditional work opportunities no longer exist. Basic literacy skills are necessary to avoid exploitation and to cope with many of the demands of society today. Now even passing a driving test, such an essential skill for a Traveller, requires taking a written theory paper.

In the mid 1980s I conducted a series of interviews with Gypsy Traveller parents about their attitudes to education. I could not at that time persuade any of them to attend an in-service training session for teachers and give their views in person (though several have done so since), but they were willing to speak on tape for me to replay to other teachers.

Some of the parents wished their children to have greater opportunities than they had been offered themselves:

> I want to give them what I never had – a proper education. It's the only place they can get it – in school – they can't get it from us because none of us can read nor write. (Kiddle 1984, interview transcripts)

> I just wanted him to learn to read and write and to be educated. Well I've had no education. (ibid.)

Some felt it was important for the children to mix with non-Gypsies and that they had the right to the same opportunities:

> Why should they be classed different? I don't want my children to be separate. My children are as good as them. They're as good as the other children. (ibid.)

> I'd like them to learn to read and write just like any other child, but they've got to learn there's other people in the world as well. She's got to learn how to get on with others... playing with gauje children she's going to learn their ways as well as our own. (ibid.)

Others again wanted straightforward skill acquisition.

> To read and write. Cooking they know that from watching all the
> time.... It's no good for us to learn the way you people live, because
> there's no call for it in our way of life... to learn to read and write
> would be a big help. When they're travelling the roads to look at the
> sign posts to tell them which way to go. (ibid.)

> The most important thing for us is reading... we educate ourselves, but
> a little bit of reading and writing helps us in our work as well... school
> is very important in that way... when I went to school, after I learnt to
> read and write they couldn't teach anything else to me. (ibid.)

It was, in 1976 as I first experienced, and is still abundantly clear that a concern
for their children to achieve basic literacy is the overwhelming motive for which
Gypsy and Traveller parents put their children into school in the first place. But
for some there is further motivation as there is a recognition of a changing
world and a desire to throw off the years of discrimination and denial of
opportunity.

However, there is still no automatic assumption of school attendance, the
access has so often been limited or denied that family education has had to be
sufficient and this responsibility has been accepted and followed through.
There will be many occasions when family affairs will take precedence over
school attendance. Recently an extended family group of Irish Travellers came
into my area to celebrate a wedding. It proved possible to arrange with the priest
that some of the children could take their first communions at the end of the
following week. The children had done the basic preparation necessary, but the
families had not been able to stop anywhere for long enough for them to make
their first communions. With the co-operation of the Gypsy Liaison Officer the
families were able to stay on the field where they were for an extra week and
everything went ahead – except for school attendance. In the first week
everyone was too busy with the excitement of the wedding preparations to
organise getting the children ready for school; in the second week there were
similar activities for the communions, clothes to buy and so on. As soon as the
ceremonies were over the families were obliged to move on. School places were
available in this area from the beginning of the first week when the families
arrived, but the importance of and preparations for the family social and
religious events came first. This kind of prioritising will always be the case when
family education is considered more stable and of more importance than
schooling. This will especially be the case where there are anxieties about the
reception the children will have in school or where there is little confidence in
the value of a schooling which is constantly interrupted, with no possibility of
any kind of continuity.

As we saw in the last chapter parents continue to have anxieties about
sending children to school to a potentially hostile environment – worries about

their own rejection at the headteacher's or the secretary's door, worries about the children being subject to bullying and name-calling, worries about their being away from the protection of the family and possibly picking up unwelcome attitudes and values from their peer group, worries about health scares and accidents (particularly on school trips, when the parents will not always know precisely where the children are). Some Gypsy Traveller parents who have had some schooling themselves have too many bad memories of unpleasant experiences in their own school days, when they were made to feel inadequate, inappropriately dressed and unwelcome, to let their own children go easily to school.

Susie, a young Traveller woman in her twenties clearly remembers incidents at primary school in the early 1980s:

> When I was young we were in London and I went to about ten different schools. I didn't like it, I don't know why... but we were always moving and I was never anywhere more than a few weeks. I never had a chance in any one school.... I've been to some schools where I wasn't welcome. I'll give you an example. We were stopping at the Angel in London and when we went into this school we had our own class – for the Travelling children – and then each day we'd be put in the class we were supposed to be in. One day we were walking into the playground. There was a wire mesh fence on the path up to the playground and there was a bit of a wall and the playground was up high. All the other children in the school were lined up against this fence and they were screaming at us. We were standing there on this path and we had to be walked into the playground by the teachers.... Some children in the schools you could play with, but others just called you names. When I was smaller it was easier. (Kiddle 1997, interview transcript)

All these fears about what might and sometimes does happen to children once in school that I have touched on here and given consideration to in the previous chapter are intensely important to Gypsy Traveller parents. Important to all parents, of course, but to an ethnic minority group who experience hostility daily in the outside world and who may have no reason to expect anything different in school, much more so. When children themselves have expressed anxieties or attitudes about school, which have confirmed parents' own fears or assumptions, the children have not been forced to attend. Parents' fears were found to have justification in the 1985 Swann Report: 'In many respects the situation in which Travellers' children find themselves also illustrates to an extreme degree the experience of prejudice and alienation which faces many other ethnic minority children' (DES 1985).

That Gypsy Traveller parents do send their children to school in increasing numbers despite all this, demonstrates the extent to which it is now being recognised that school education needs to take its place alongside that of the family.

The Swann report also confirms the preoccupation of this chapter:

> Whereas, with the other groups of children whom we have considered,
> we have been chiefly concerned with their needs within schools, many
> of the particular educational needs of Travellers' children arise because
> of difficulties in gaining access to the education system at all. (ibid.)

The substance of this chapter has been to look at these difficulties for access, which remain substantially unchanged thirteen years after the publication of the Swann Report, and at some of the strategies developed for overcoming them. Those parents who have recognised how the economic changes and the developing sophistication of the communications systems in the wider society must inevitably affect and impinge on their own ways of life, have sought out teachers and schools to help them to equip their children for the future. The education system has responded and worked proactively to open the doors wider and encourage entry. But settled society is not giving a simple message to Gypsy Traveller parents. As schools and teachers increasingly offer a welcome and a respect for a minority culture, many neighbourhoods continue to evict and reject. Government policy pushes onwards reducing the accommodation options other than housing and settlement. It must be difficult for parents to believe that anything other than assimilation is sought. Those parents who do consider that letting their children imbibe the culture and values of the non-Traveller society through school will result in a gradual disintegration of their own culture and that this outweighs the perceived benefits of school education, have found many strategies to keep their children out of school. This is most noticeable at secondary level, which will be discussed more fully in a later chapter.

This chapter has looked at questions of access in legal, practical and motivational terms that allow the realisation of the child's rights to an education as in Articles 28 and 29 of the UN Convention on the Rights of the Child. Gypsy Traveller children have been enrolled in ever increasing numbers in primary schools to acquire functional literacy. Their parents often overcome severe practical difficulties in order to get them there. After a good deal of effort from many quarters, despite the obstacles put up by others, understanding has grown and relationships of trust have been built up between teachers and parents to a certain degree. Yet always the power differential will affect the relationship in some way. Teachers and parents have established the rights and enabled the access of many Traveller children to primary school. The children are now discovering if it has been worth it. Whilst many are made welcome and efforts are made to give them an equal opportunity in school, too many still, like Johnny and Susie can have a bad experience.

CHAPTER FOUR

Parents' Rights and Children's Rights

There is an ambivalence in Gypsy Traveller parents' attitudes to state school education. There is no doubt that when they put their children into schools it is primarily so that they will learn to read and write and there can often be considerable frustration for these parents and the children if this is not seen to happen in a relatively short period of time. Beyond the opportunity to acquire these skills many parents see little relevance in schooling and others consider it potentially harmful to the structure of their society which is based on an understanding and acceptance of certain roles and responsibilities within the family group. Some successful, non-literate Gypsy Travellers even cast doubt on the uses of literacy and its possible consequences for their oral traditions. It is a commonplace in conversation to hear: 'When you learn to read and write you lose your memory'.

In these circumstances some Gypsy Traveller parents exercise their right to educate their children themselves out of school, either from the time that the children reach school age, or more commonly at the time of transfer to secondary education or when they have reached a certain level of competence in reading and writing. It is certainly their legal right to do so. As stated in an earlier chapter the 1944 Education Act gives parents the responsibility of ensuring that their children receive an efficient full time education 'by regular attendance at school or otherwise' (DES 1944) and gives LEAs the duty to monitor the effectiveness of the arrangements made. It is this decision by some Gypsy and also other Traveller parents to offer their children 'education otherwise' that this chapter will begin by considering. Although the right to educate your children otherwise than at school has been lawful since the 1944 Act, it is only comparatively recently that this option has become more generally and widely known among Gypsy Traveller families.

It is possible that the promotion of home schooling by New Traveller support groups such as the Travellers School Charity has contributed to this increased awareness. The young people, some couples with children, who came out from housing to begin to live nomadic lives in the late 1960s and through the 1970s and 1980s all had their own separate and individual reasons for taking to life on the roads. However, the extensive media coverage around 1985 with the confrontations at Stonehenge and the so-called 'battle of the beanfield' soon spawned collective names – New Age Travellers, Hippy Convoy, Mediaeval Brigands etc. – and created a new negative stereotype. For some a travelling life was a deliberate and positive choice, a desire to do things differently, a reaction against materialism, a 'green' statement. For others it was forced – a broken relationship, a flight from abuse, a social or economic rejection by the wider society. For some it was a complete alienation from a system which they felt had failed them. For many, to turn back to the state to educate their children for them was not an acceptable option. They wished to educate their children themselves. In part it was a practical, in part intellectual, in part emotional response to the situation in which they found themselves. I knew from my own experience in the early 1970s how difficult it was to relate to the regular school system whilst travelling.

A significant number of the New Travellers were educated, intelligent and articulate. They knew education law and their right to choose education at home and formed a self-help group, later the Travellers School Charity, to support each other and lobby at local, regional and national level. Their activities became increasingly organised and known to other groups of Travellers.

The knowledge that 'Education Otherwise' (EO) is a parents' right to choose has certainly led to an increase in the declarations by Gypsy Traveller parents of their intention to exercise this right (OFSTED 1996, p.26 para. 70). Whether they fulfil their obligations to their children, having once formally taken on this responsibility, will obviously vary from family to family, and there has to be scope for considerable debate about what to 'fulfil their obligations to their children' means when viewed from different cultural perspectives.

Gypsy Traveller families who have not wanted their children in school, for whatever reason, have always found ways of avoiding it. Teachers of Travelling children and Education Welfare Officers will all be familiar with comments like, 'No shoes', 'We're shifting on Sunday', 'She's gone to her granny', 'He's with his uncle in Germany', 'We're moving tomorrow'. Such excuses as these are made from a position of understanding that school attendance is compulsory and that prosecution for non-attendance is possible. Parents are now increasingly aware that education outside school is a legal choice for them to make. For many generations Gypsy Traveller parents, with limited access to mainstream schools, had no real option but to educate their children themselves. Now that access and the children's right to an equal educational opportunity as all other children is beginning to be assured, it would be a pity if parents refused it on their children's behalf from a fear or a lack of accurate knowledge of what is on offer.

Parents, both Traveller and non-Traveller, come to the decision to educate their children 'otherwise' than at school from several different perspectives. Some deliberately assert that right in a wholly positive way. They know the school system, they know their child, they have planned their family's social circumstances and daily routines to accommodate the child being at home and they believe that they are themselves best equipped to give the child what they perceive it needs. They may have academic, religious, social or cultural reasons for their choice. Non-Traveller families have been making this choice for many years. Many of us became familiar through wide publicity with the case of Ruth Lawrence in the late 1970s when she won a place at Oxford University to read maths before she had entered her teens. Her father, seeing a gifted child with a precocious talent made an academic choice and kept her at home, tutoring her himself. Her academic success cannot be denied. Other families positively take the decision to keep their children out of school for religious reasons so that they can be assured that their child is having the religious teaching and upbringing that they desire and that this will not conflict with other teaching that the school might give. They do not necessarily have total confidence in their abilities to offer a full academic curriculum and often these parents will welcome the support and advice they receive from LEA advisers and inspectors who have the statutory duty to monitor the adequacy of provision of education other than at school.

Some Gypsy and other Traveller parents also make the education otherwise decision in a positive way, choosing to educate their children within their own cultural group and bringing in tuition from the outside to cover areas that they feel are necessary, but that they cannot offer from their own capabilities. Save the Children project workers felt the strength of this feeling which was recorded in their report on child rearing in a Gypsy Traveller community:

> Some...Travellers believe that during adolescence the major lessons are to be learned from parents, not from schools. The most important thing to learn was 'tradition, the way of life, the way we go on'. The Traveller way of life was central. (Arnold *et al.* 1992, p.22)

As long as the rights of the child can be protected by the safeguard of LEA monitoring the parents are free to make their choice. That all these parents have taken into account and variously compensated for the social, emotional and academic consequences of isolating their children from their contemporaries in school needs to be ensured. Parents positively opting for EO can also take advantage of organisations such as the one named Education Otherwise and the Travellers School Charity, which are specifically set up to support those with home schooling arrangements.

There are other parents who opt for EO in a negative way. That is to say that they have knowledge of the school system from their own experience as pupils and have decided that they do not want their children to share that experience. I have met several New Traveller families who came to EO in this way, who have generalised negative attitudes towards all schools from their own particular schooldays in one or two institutions. Unhappy personal school experiences have been added to other rejections and compounded feelings of alienation leading to a determination to keep their own children as far as possible from all state institutions and control. Choosing the freedom from school they then have to confront the reality of educating the children themselves. This can be extremely difficult while living a nomadic life as so much time is inevitably taken up in the daily routines of survival – finding water, collecting wood, dealing with the insecurities of unauthorised stopping places which may be hidden away far from shops, launderettes and other facilities. Parents in this situation rarely have adequate time or resources for the daily repetition, reinforcement and staged progress needed for teaching basic literacy and numeracy skills. Some struggle along as best as they can, seeking help and materials from Traveller Education Services or Traveller charities and voluntary organisations. Others reject the idea of the need for any kind of formal teaching and embrace the generalised concepts of 'learning from life' and 'learning by doing', trusting that the necessary skills will somehow be picked up by their children along the way. Some renege on their responsibilities or question the need for literacy at all, pointing to evidently successful and capable non-literate Gypsy Travellers.

It is interesting to compare attitudes like these to those of Gypsy Travellers. As has been described in earlier chapters of this book, the majority of Gypsy Traveller parents, though brought up in a largely non-literate society themselves, though knowing how to cope, how to survive and succeed without reading, are now bringing their children to schools precisely because they feel that in today's society reading and writing are essential skills. Yet some literate New Travellers, who will not have the coping and compensating skills of the non-literate to pass on to their children, do not consider literacy a high priority. It is unlikely that the rights to a full education of the children in these circumstances will be protected by LEA monitoring. Those who are alienated from education systems are unlikely to register themselves as home-schoolers in the first place and those who do come to the notice of LEA officials will probably use mobility as a strategy for avoiding unwelcome intrusion by the authorities. It seems a pity to change the emphasis from the desirability of learning one set of skills to another, when it should be possible, given the co-operation of parents and teachers, to gain both literacy skills and practical knowledge in a range of areas of activity. In this context it is interesting to read accounts of their experiences written by New Travellers who have gone abroad to pursue nomadic ways of life (Dearling 1998), and hear how many bureaucratic procedures must be followed to get a work permit in France and how much better it is to travel in France and Spain with some knowledge of the language of the country.

Other than choosing EO positively or negatively, some parents arrive there by a less informed third route. This is a way that is ignorant of the alternatives or is based only on fears or hearsay about what goes on in schools. I have talked with several New Traveller parents who on first encounter stated quite emphatically that they were educating their children themselves. When it became clear through conversation that I came from a support service, not an enforcement agency, the attitudes would shift, the worries about not feeling able to cope adequately with home education would surface, the anxieties about what might happen if children were registered in school would be revealed. It was not schools or formal education *per se* which were being rejected, but there were a plethora of worries about possible bullying or victimisation, about harassment by officials if children were once registered but then turned out to be only intermittent attenders, about a lack of understanding of their lifestyle and the lack of respect for their cultural values.

It is these kinds of diffuse anxieties that I believe also influence many of the Gypsy Traveller parents in opting for EO for their children, particularly at the stage of transfer to secondary level. The families often do not have accurate, up to date information about secondary education and all that it offers and entails on which to base a choice, but most certainly they do have a myriad of fearful imaginings. The whole issue of Travellers and secondary education will be looked at in another chapter; the concern here is that with the knowledge of EO as a legal alternative to schooling, some families are tempted to follow this route without making a fully informed choice. In doing so they can cut their children off not only from what schools can offer, but also from the various levels of information, advice and support that are set up to ease the way through. In these circumstances parents' rights and children's rights do not sit easily together.

When I was travelling with my family as part of the theatre group (as described in the first chapter of this book), we found ourselves *de facto* doing Education Otherwise as we found that it was the only practical solution to our full touring schedule. England could not offer a school of distance education on a par with the Australian model which will be described in a later chapter. When I went to the local education office to register our intention and ask if there was any help available, I was told that we could choose to educate the children ourselves, but that would cut us off from state education support, facilities and resources. There was no mention of monitoring our progress and I can only assume that this was because the official did not think this would be possible with a travelling group. At the time I was pleased that they were letting us get on with it ourselves without undue fuss or harassment, it was only later that the full responsibility of it dawned. It is only now that I worry about what the lack of monitoring could have meant for the group's children if we had been irresponsible or not taken their educational needs seriously. What we did in effect was to use every resource, human and material, that we had available and try to make a coherence of the children's lives within a working theatre group.

When my family left the group and had completed the action research work for ACERT and the Romany Guild at the end of 1976, we returned to settled jobs and a house-dwelling existence and we were faced with the prospect of putting our son into the local village school. At first I did not want to do it. I had grown used to building his education into our working lives and I was loath to let other people start to shape his attitudes and his values and felt that his development would be out of my control. Nevertheless living now isolated in a small nuclear family I did not believe that we could offer him enough on our own. I wrote about it at the time:

> I did not want to lose my son to school, but when I thought about the facilities offered by the small base of one household, there was no comparison with the resources available at school. I considered joining with other families in another co-operative education venture, but there was no centre to work round, as the theatre company had been. A base, a starting point was necessary, and it soon became obvious that the base already existed in the local school. There the resources were already concentrated, there all the families from six neighbouring villages already came together, with the financial backing of the government. There my son would be part of his local community, not isolated from it. This was vitally important as the village network was undoubtedly one of the best resources of the area. To ignore it would be ridiculous. (Kiddle 1981, p.108–109)

I put my son into school, but took care to get involved with many of the school activities so that I still felt I was sharing in his education and not relinquishing the responsibility totally to the teachers.

We did not live in the village where the school was. Some fifteen years before we moved there a new primary school had been built in the largest village in the neighbourhood and five tiny schools in the surrounding villages were closed down. All the children were bussed into the new school. Our village only had a few young children resident at the time and my son was one of just six in his age group who travelled into school together on the bus each day. Five of them were boys and there was one girl. As it has turned out every one of the families of those six children has remained living in the village and I have been able to keep in touch with the little group who went to primary school together and are now in their early twenties. The six children had the same state schooling, all went through the village primary school and then on to the large comprehensive community college in the nearest town which served the whole of the rural area. Yet beyond their formal schooling their several parents gave them hugely different other skills and experiences. One learned to ride, to shoot, to breed animals; one spent nearly all his out of school time in a boat; one joined group after group – church groups, red cross groups, sea scouts groups; one learned circus skills and went busking; two others including the girl, were completely involved in their family farming and building businesses and the social life of the village. The three whose parents were incomers to the neighbourhood when the children were small, have travelled widely in England and abroad, the other three, from long established local families, have rarely been out of the county. The three whose parents had had higher education went on themselves to universities. The other three had further education and training locally. All six are now either working within their family businesses or are studying or in work in areas similar to those which their parents followed.

Recently I had a discussion with a New Traveller mother, living in a truck on farmland, quite determined to educate her own children. She was delighting in the closeness to nature that her children had, that they could care for animals, that they knew wild flowers and birdsong. She was working on their reading, which she also considered essential, and she could see no need to send them to school. More than this she believed that school would somehow blunt their sensitivity to their surroundings. For me it does not have to be a question of either/or. What one aspect of life gives does not necessarily preclude a gain from another, nor inevitably diminish it – the parent has a vital role in integrating the two for the children.

In the case of the group of children from my own village, it is clear to see the family circumstances and influences which shaped these children's lives so differently one from another from the base of a full and identical state school attendance. I look at these families, not all of them particularly strong extended families and see the parental influence at work, not necessarily a pressure, but a modelling and something of an expectation. I think of Gypsy Traveller parents, often worried that schooling will, by providing other opportunities and a different peer pressure, break down the family influence and erode their culture and I feel that they need not have such anxieties. Where the family base is strong, and for most Gypsy Traveller families it is central, that influence will, I am convinced, remain paramount. In a recent video a clear statement comes from an eighteen-year-old Gypsy Traveller girl, studying for her 'A' levels in a sixth form college: 'I'd like to meet someone who would dare to tell me I'm not a Traveller any more!' (DfEE, *Are We Missing Out?* 1998).

Parents do have the power and do have rights to choose to educate their children entirely themselves, but I believe that parents should have confidence in the power of their own influence and be open to others providing opportunities and skills for their children that they cannot give. To deny those possibilities because they are felt to be threatening is I believe unnecessary and denies the children's rights to a full education. Such rights are outlined in Paragraph 1 (a) of Article 29 of the UN Convention on the Rights of the Child, which makes clear the child's right to an education directed to the development of the child's personality and the realisation of his or her full potential.

Because of the marginalisation and prejudice which Gypsy Traveller groups have faced through successive generations, they have consciously sought to raise their children to be able to cope with the sundry effects of discrimination.

> My observations have led me to conclude that the ways in which Travellers raise their children, often produce self-confident young people, with skills, abilities and competences in some areas of their lives, which are very advanced compared to their peers in the settled community. I believe this is very necessary for their survival as

> members of their own community but also because they confront open
> hostility and prejudice from the settled community. (Arnold *et al.*
> 1992, p.16)

Gypsy Traveller parents will continue to do this. There is not yet an automatic
assumption of school attendance as I have said before. They will only put their
children into school willingly if they consider that the extra skills, of whatever
sort, that can be gained there are worth having. These will be balanced against
any perceived disadvantage or threat, a consideration of whether their own
cultural values are being reinforced or countered.

> Education by the institutions of the sedentary society can be viewed as
> a vehicle by which the cultural norms of the dominant group are
> imposed on the marginal group; it may also influence the nature of
> gender roles within the family. Since school attendance removes
> children from the spatial arena of the 'homeplace' and its cultural
> influence, education can be perceived as a form of cultural
> assimilation.... Education can also, however, be seen as a way that the
> community, via literacy, can gain skills in order to access resources
> denied them by the dominant society due to their non-literacy.
> (Kendall 1997, p.86)

Traveller families who put their children into schools continue to maintain their
own cultural priorities alongside, and studies of school attendance patterns
demonstrate that events that serve to confirm the community identity will take
precedence over school attendance, just as the wedding and first communions
did as described in the preceding chapter.

> It is apparent that Travellers are indicating, despite the demand for
> continuous attendance at a non-Traveller institution, the paramountcy
> for them of the recognition of the importance of the celebration of
> such occasions...(visiting relatives, weddings, funerals, other social
> and economic functions).... The causes of absence identified by the
> Traveller sample interviewed serve to reinforce self identity and
> demarcate them from majority society. Their cohesion and survival as a
> people is therefore promoted by their children's immersion in such
> observances. (Clay 1997, p.156)

I witnessed a young Gypsy Traveller boy facing a real dilemma. He was in his
second year at the secondary school and seeming really to enjoy it. He could
cope academically in his class and was a good and keen sportsman, which had
helped him to integrate socially into non-Traveller friendship groups though he
continued also to associate closely with other Travellers in the school. He was
quite delighted when he was picked to play in the school football team and his
mother supported his success and made sure he always had the appropriate kit.
Unfortunately the day of the first match in which he was to play away from
school clashed with the main day of the October horse fair at Stow which the

family always attended. He struggled to decide where his loyalties lay, but finally he was not given a personal choice. His father said that there was no question but that he would go to the fair with the rest of the family.

Any child has to be strong to stand up and make their own choices when their inclinations conflict with family expectations, even more so when the choices are not made simply in the context of child/parent power relationships but can be seen to affect the solidarity of the family group and its relationship to the dominant society. I recently interviewed an elderly Gypsy Traveller woman, who recalled for me her struggles when she was determined to get a school education. Before the Second World War her family had travelled through the south west of England with horses and waggons, returning each winter to the same area, where her father would rent a field from a local farmer for a few months and the children would go to school. After the war her father decided to settle in their winter area, bought a field and put a chalet on to it for the family to live in. She was eleven years old by this time and started at the secondary school. I asked if her parents had been happy to let her go to the secondary school:

> They had to… when you settled down the school board would come. Your parents thought you'd be more use at home – we were needed at home – but I was determined that when I left school I was going out to work, I didn't want to go round to the doors, I didn't want to do that…. We had to learn the hard way and school wasn't easy either. The other children would bully you and I think it made you tough. They'd call you names and look down on you and the clothes you wore and everything like that and even some of the teachers. I had some very nice teachers – you remember those – but there were some that were not so nice. It was difficult. At home when you'd pick up a book and read your parents would say – 'Well what are you doing that for?' That's what my dad would say, 'That's not going to keep you', he'd say, 'What's the point of learning to read?' But thank God I did learn to read… I had a good teacher, Miss Hunter, and well, I came second in the class. I was interested in school work and I did pretty well… I've always wanted to read and find out about things…. The headmaster saw my dad but I had to leave at 14… I didn't really want to do the things that mum and dad could do… so I went out and got a job in shops at various places and I always got promotion wherever I was… my dad just accepted it after a while because he knew I wasn't going to do what he wanted me to do…. It was a difficult life for all of us because our fathers and mothers were so strict. They didn't like you wearing make-up at all and dresses not too short… if you went out they'd want to know where you are, they were protective. My dad used to come and meet me every day from work to make sure I got home alright…. I think he realised…he didn't want us to face the hardships that he'd had to face in his family… life wasn't easy. (Kiddle 1997, interview transcript)

Even more recently I met the young Gypsy Traveller girl, who spoke so clearly in the video *Are We Missing Out?*, when she was in the sixth form of her school in Cambridgeshire and making applications to university to study law. Since she was four years old, she said, she has wanted to be a solicitor and her strength of purpose has been such that her parents have supported her. She has been fully integrated in her school though it has not been easy. She believes that the three way relationship between herself, her parents and her teachers has been essential to keeping her going. She stressed how difficult it was for children to cope with mainstream school on their own and how necessary support from both parents and teachers was.

A few years ago another teenage Gypsy Traveller girl, after only spending a couple of terms in secondary school at the age of eleven, took up a training course in computing and word-processing skills when she was sixteen. A capable and intelligent girl, she gained the qualification easily and completed over eight months work experience in an office placement. She described her experience:

> At first I liked it, but I got bored with it after a while and I hated that you were inside. It was the middle of summer, a hot summer and I wasn't used to being inside all the time. I was in this little office, inside the factory and it never had a window or anything… I went milk, snowy white and I got headaches because of the light…. I left there and got a different placement in an insurance office. That was alright and they asked me to stay on after the work experience and they would pay me full wages until they got someone else to take my place…. I did stay on for a while, but they never gave me the full wages, so I left…. I started going out with my dad doing the knifegrinding. I prefer doing the sharpening because when I was in the little office I was on my own. Out with my dad I'm outside and meeting people…. I've been going out with my dad for about six or seven years now. I thought I might go to college and do a beauty course. If we were going to stop here – say if mum and dad settled then probably I would…. I wouldn't do office work again…. I know I can go and learn something at any time. If I really wanted to do something I would have the confidence to go down and see about it. (Kiddle 1997, interview transcript)

Several points seem worth drawing out of this account. Although the girl dropped out of secondary school very early, she was sufficiently literate to be quite capable of fulfilling the training course requirements in a college environment a few years later. Her family supported her throughout. Though her father was very pleased when she started to work with him within the family economic unit, he was prepared for her to experience other work. The employer exploited her, probably well aware that she would not know how to initiate complaints procedures. Though working within the family business at present she is quite prepared to take up other opportunities as they become available.

This is a story of our times; family and school/college education have combined to give this young Traveller woman a range of options. She has been brought up with the support of both parents and teachers to have the confidence to take up what she chooses for herself. Yet her first and immediate experience of an employer was one of exploitation. It is the belief that even with education and qualifications the Gypsy Traveller will still be discriminated against in employment that keeps many families determinedly self-employed and anxious to give their children their own ways of surviving. It leads others to deny their identities and heritage.

Other parents are concerned that if the young women are too independent they will not find a marriage easily within their community. Some families fear that for the children to have a range of options will inevitably lead to a weakening of the acceptance of traditional roles and responsibilities within the family. This still motivates many Gypsy Traveller parents to deny secondary schooling to their children, particularly the girls. I have had many discussions with parents about this issue trying to understand the deep cultural anxiety and different cultural attitudes from my own on questions relating to gender. It always seems strange to me that parents who will not let their children into schools for fear that they may pick up other values and start on the road towards assimilation, yet have television and video players in their trailers and allow fairly unrestricted viewing. To me the pervasive power of mass media can be a stronger force than the ethos of any individual school and contributes to the process of the continuing change within all our cultures. Evidently the girls are considered vulnerable and open to exploitation in school and their physical protection is paramount. This is coupled with the determination by some parents that an acceptance of domestic responsibilities will be maintained.

The balance of children's rights and parents' rights shifted in UK law with the Children Act in 1989. The overriding principles contained in the Act were that the best interests of the child should be the first consideration and that the voice of the child should be heard.

Children's rights were now to be seen clearly in the context of parental responsibility. The principles of the Children Act are very close to those set out in the UN Convention on the Rights of the Child which the UK government signed in 1990. There is little evidence so far that Gypsy and Traveller children's rights are being particularly picked up as an issue. In February 1994 the UK published its first report to the UN Committee on the Rights of the Child. In England there is no specific mention of Gypsy or Traveller groups; in the sections concerning minority groups it is Section 11 and language issues that predominate. In response to Article 30 in which it is stated that every person has the right to enjoy his or her own culture, religion and language, it is only in the Northern Ireland context that Irish Travellers are included:

Among issues likely to emerge are some which may particularly concern children and young persons in ethnic minority communities, including traditional Irish Travellers. These include abuse and harassment, social isolation, problems in respect of educational attainment, difficulty in accessing social services and lack of adequate child care facilities. (HMSO 1994)

It is to be welcomed that in continuing an Advisory Group set up by the Conservative government to look at ways of raising the educational achievement of ethnic minority pupils, the new Labour government in 1997 included Gypsy Travellers. In the circumstances in which Gypsy Traveller children find themselves, it cannot only be a parental responsibility to ensure their educational entitlement.

Some Gypsy Traveller parents, when questioned about their responsibility to ensure their children receive full-time education, will say that their children do not want to attend school and they will not force their children into situations where they have clearly voiced their opinion against it. It is difficult to accept this reasoning from families who in other circumstances, in dealing with family issues, will certainly expect children to behave and act as they are told to and personal inclinations will not be a consideration. In a community where parents make certain demands and have clear expectations of their children's responsibilities to the family group, a laxity about ensuring school attendance says more about parental anxiety than respect for a child's right to be heard. It is an abnegation of responsibility which uses young children themselves as an excuse.

Finally it is about power. The ability and willingness for Gypsy Traveller parents to allow their children to take up their rights to full educational opportunities in school will be affected by the power relationships that exist between them and the sedentary society. At every moment and in every situation Gypsy Travellers are conscious of the power relations with the 'host' society, their identity is bound up as much in what they are not as what they are, in what they reject as what they choose. Gypsy culture and non-Gypsy culture cannot be seen in isolation from each other any more than either can remain static. 'Gypsy culture inhabits and constructs its internal coherence alongside or in opposition to other dominating cultures in the same geographical and political space' (Okely 1997, p.189).

In his study of the narrative folklore of the travelling people of Scotland, Donald Braid maintains that whenever non-Travellers are present at a Traveller narrative event, the dynamic of the relationship itself will be brought out in some way. 'When interaction narratives are performed in events with non-Traveller participants, both the dynamics of the narrative event and the narrative content become particularly relevant to understanding cross cultural negotiations of identity. In these events, issues of cultural identity are frequently foregrounded' (Braid 1997, p.46).

The consciousness of the relationship is always there. I was reminded of it forcibly very recently when I telephoned a Gypsy Traveller woman whom I know well one evening. The phone was answered and I said just three words 'Is Louie there?' The phone had been answered by a young daughter who did not know me so well and who would not immediately recognise my voice, but in my accent and tone of voice she heard all that was immediately important to her. I heard her call across the trailer to her mother saying, 'It's a gauje'. Whoever it was, whatever the content of the call was going to be, the Gypsy/gauje relationship would be there as the base.

There is a determination by the minority group that finally in any given situation they will not be forced by the dominating majority to act in a way they do not choose. Always Gypsy Traveller groups hold on to the ultimate possibility of mobility as an escape, even those who have been housed or notionally settled for years. In her study of school attendance patterns of Traveller children in Wales, Sandra Clay concludes:

> Policies promoting assimilation and coercion have come to be seen as inappropriate. Support offered via the operation of the county specialist service has proved effective. Essentially progress has been made only with the co-operative partnership of Traveller families and schools. Where Traveller identity and culture is respected it is self-evident that attendance will continue to improve. (Clay 1997, p.157)

In Ireland George Gmelch's studies confirmed that those Travellers who seemed to have decided to settle in housing would leave on an instant if they found themselves facing difficulties that they were not prepared to tolerate (Gmelch 1985). Jean Pierre Liégeois too (Liégeois 1994) emphasises that Roma and Gypsy Traveller peoples throughout Europe, even after years of perhaps enforced settlement, nevertheless see mobility as an ever present possibility. A defining characteristic remains the rejection of a sedentary attitude of mind.

My own experience in England only corroborates that of others. I know a Gypsy Traveller family who had remained on an unofficial, but tolerated stopping place for over ten years, putting up with appalling living conditions but choosing to stay and fight for their rights to a decently built site. Attendance at secondary school became an issue for one of the boys. Though his parents were not against secondary school on principle and their daughters had attended for a while, the boy was adamant that he would not go. There were discussions for several months, positive visits to the school by the parents, transport and uniform arrangements, but still no attendance. The EWO finally spoke of prosecution for non-attendance and within a week the family had moved away. The site issue, the long established work contacts, were of less significance than the determination not to be compelled by the 'gauje'.

Gypsy Traveller peoples have consistently been victimised and made scapegoats in all the countries they inhabit for refusing to conform to the settled norm. Robbie McVeigh sees 'unsympathetic repression' and 'benevolent assimilation' as only 'complementary sedentary projects', which at their extreme are genocidal (McVeigh 1997). Sinéad ní Shuinéar argues that sedentary society keeps the Gypsy as a marginalised outsider because it needs the scapegoat: 'Gaujos not only (consciously, deliberately) scapegoat the Gypsy, they also (subconsciously) project onto him, thus distancing themselves from things they dislike about themselves' (ní Shuinéar 1997, p.52).

In surveys to find the most unpopular groups across Europe and America, the Gypsy is invariably the most vilified (Hancock 1997). We all see this hostility day after day, we have seen Gypsies and Travellers made victims many times, yet the Gypsy Traveller peoples have consistently refused to accept the status or have the consciousness of a victim group. At the time when I was living on a site in London with Gypsy Traveller families I would often be angry and upset at the constant name-calling and general abuse thrown at us by members of my own community. I was surprised at the seeming relative unconcern and remarkable sanity demonstrated by my neighbours in the face of all this, which they had put up with for far longer than I. I asked once why they did not get more angry and had the reply – 'Well, we know your people are rude and ignorant, there's no point in letting them get you down'. It is their very resilience in the face of attempts at repression and assimilation, often in situations of extreme vulnerability, that marks them out and keeps their identity vibrant and alive. In their daily dealings with non-Gypsy society they demonstrate a skill in the understanding and management of economic and other relationships which is hard to beat.

If the educational establishment genuinely wants education for all and is concerned that Gypsy Traveller children are able to claim their entitlement to education, able to take full advantage of what both their parents and their schools can offer in an integrated way, then the school system of the 'host' society has to pick up its share of the responsibility. It cannot only be a parents' responsibility. Schools have to be welcoming, respond to differing situations and needs with a responsive flexibility and offer a relevant curriculum. Teachers have to take on the responsibility of undertaking the necessary outreach work to discuss with parents the opportunities that schools present and the fears that they generate. Parents will not easily approach or trust an institution of a state that has alternately been repressive and assimilative in its policies over centuries and continues to be so. Unless schools are unequivocally intercultural and accepting of diversity then some parents will continue to opt for Education Otherwise and in so doing in many cases deny their children many of the skills and opportunities that they might otherwise have. The rights of the children will fall victim to the Gypsy/non-Gypsy adult power dynamic.

CHAPTER FIVE

The Child's Right to an Identity

At secondary school level, when Gypsy Traveller children reach adolescence, all the tensions created by engagement in the formal educational process, some of which have already been discussed or hinted at, are more extreme. This is the time when traditionally the parental need for the children to take part in the family work, to learn family trades and help generate income or take on greater domestic and childcare responsibilities, and the parental protective concern for the physical and moral welfare of the children all combine most strongly. The dominance of these factors contributes largely to absences from secondary school. As has already been mentioned in an earlier chapter, the 1996 OFSTED report on the education of Traveller children calculated that there are possibly as many as 10,000 such children of secondary school age who are not even registered with school.

The various attitudes and actions which affect non-attendance or irregular attendance by Gypsy Traveller children at secondary school have been considered many times, most recently by DfE 1992; Arnold *et al.* 1992; Hawes and Perez 1995; OFSTED 1996; Jordan 1996; Naylor and Wild-Smith 1997; Wrexham TES 1997; and in many other reports and case studies given at national, regional and local conferences. A summary of some of them may be helpful in understanding the situation.

Let us look at it first from the parents' point of view. Contributory reasons for Traveller parents either finding it difficult to send their children or support them in school, condoning absence or deliberately keeping children out of secondary school are both positive and negative. Parents can be anxious about:

- Children being in a potentially hostile environment and the sheer size of some secondary schools.
- Bullying and name-calling, particularly outside the relative security of the classroom.
- The children not being able to cope with the curriculum if they have poor literacy skills.
- The moral welfare of, especially, teenage girls.
- Sex education and related discussions.

- Possible access to drugs.
- Having showers and PE, with no facilities for private changing or washing.
- Health scares in schools, not necessarily the ones the children may be attending.
- The possibility of accidents on trips out of school.
- Mixing with non-Traveller pupils and picking up different values from those of the family.
- Assimilation and being educated out of their own culture.
- Potential damage to the family network if too many outside options are available to children.

Some of these anxieties are common to both the primary and secondary phases, but can contribute in a cumulative way to non-attendance at secondary school.

Apart from the anxieties about school, there are also positive factors which make some parents wish to keep teenage children at home:

- Feeling that from twelve or thirteen years of age children need a family education, to understand and take on roles and responsibilities within the family to ensure its continuing strength.
- The economic need for children to be part of generating the family income and to learn to make a living for themselves.
- The social/cultural desire for girls to take on more domestic responsibilities and care for younger siblings.
- The need to take part in family social, cultural and religious events (visits to fairs, weddings, funerals, Christian conventions etc.), which also affects primary attendance.

There are other attitudes and difficulties too:

- Difficulties in providing quiet space and time for homework.
- Difficulties in providing the correct uniform and PE kit (where families are mobile) and keeping up with the washing on sites where there are few facilities.
- A belief that there is no relevance for their children in a secondary curriculum once they can read and write.
- A belief that secondary education is primarily geared to taking examinations and being prepared for a job market, which has little relevance to a culture whose pride is in handed on skills, practical on the job training and self-employment.
- A belief that there will be discrimination in employment for a Gypsy Traveller even with qualifications.

Looking at all these contributory factors listed in this way you can begin to wonder how it is that any of the children go to secondary school at all. Any combination of these factors may influence the attitudes of Gypsy Traveller families who have relatively secure and stable accommodation and regular travelling patterns. They will be equally pertinent to families who are in housing or rarely travel. Those who are highly mobile or who have no legal place to stop have all the added difficulties of access which have been detailed in other chapters. Whilst it is possible to go in and out of primary schools on a short-term basis with a good deal of co-operation and good will between parents, schools and support services, at secondary level the whole process is infinitely more complicated.

That some Gypsy Traveller children do go into secondary schools, and that the numbers, although low, are slowly increasing, is partly due to changing attitudes of parents, a greater understanding of the educational opportunities offered and the need to take them up in a changing world, and partly due to proactive work by schools and Traveller Education Services. There are many strategies which have been adopted over the last decade to promote secondary school attendance, many positive actions taken and positive attitudes developed. They are well documented elsewhere by Jordan (1996) and Wrexham TES (1997) among others and rather than retread territory that will be familiar to many I will simply offer another list here for the convenience of general readers and to use as the basis for further reflection.

Some positive attitudes and actions that have been successful in promoting secondary school attendance are:

- Sensitive outreach work by EWOs, TES staff and schools, building relationships and understanding and discussing anxieties particularly at the stage of transfer to secondary school.

- Good direct communications between families and schools taking into account varying degrees of literacy among parents. Offering help with form filling etc.

- Sensitivity to individual family feelings about the children being identified as Gypsy Travellers.

- Realistic transport policies.

- Swift record exchange for mobile families and the provision of distance learning work where this will aid continuity of school education.

- An inclusive welcoming ethos within the school.

- Support in understanding the new subjects, timetables and routines of secondary school.

- Flexibility about uniform policies, wearing of jewellery, showers and changing for PE.

- Discussions with parents about the sex/drug education which may be given within the school, giving them the choice to withdraw their children if they wish.

- A good pastoral system in which a child can identify a person that they can turn to for support.

- The inclusion of Traveller perspectives within the curriculum.

- School resources which reflect, respect and include all cultures.

- Staff development sessions with both teaching and non-teaching staff to prevent unnecessary misunderstandings and raise expectations and consciousness.

- Anticipating and avoiding the creation of situations which might provoke confrontations.

- In class support for individuals or groups of children where necessary.

- Differentiated work where appropriate to open the curriculum.

- Development of peer group support and mentoring.

- Clear, enforced school policies for equal opportunities and dealing with bullying and racism.

- Concerned, swift follow up of unexplained absence.

- Clear, stable structures for children to work within when they change schools regularly or irregularly.

- Demonstration of the relevance of curriculum subjects to everyday life.

- Making sure that families know about the range of courses and options now available at 14 plus, for instance work experience, GNVQ and college attendance.

- Development of youth clubs and groups for Traveller pupils.

- Continuing discussion, negotiation and support.

So where does all this leave the children? Some undoubtedly share their parents' anxieties about what can be seen as an overwhelmingly frightening prospect, but others have their own agendas, which can conflict with those of their parents. Many times I have seen disappointment on children's faces when, worried about their safety, their parents have refused permission for them to go on a trip out of school with their class to extend curriculum work. For the parents it would mean a further extension of trust. Whilst they may be content for the children to attend school when they know where they are and can contact or collect them at any time if this should prove to be necessary, say in the event of a sudden eviction, to lose that control can be, for some parents, one step too far. From the children's point of view, they are not only sad to miss the trip itself, but also they know that in the next days at school they will not be able to understand or contribute to the follow-up work, aware that they will be marked as different, outside the group again.

Teenage girls, kept out of school by their parents because they do not want their daughters to mix with others thought to have been brought up with more permissive attitudes, have asked me to talk to them about issues that would have been naturally covered within sex education and in the PSME curriculum. They do not feel able to speak freely to or ask direct questions of their mothers, but are sometimes desperate for the most basic information. Other teenagers, also kept out of school primarily because of parental fears about what they might be exposed to, know perfectly well that drugs of all kinds are more widely available outside school than in. These children see their protection by their parents as unnecessarily restrictive.

For others it is very different. A boy whose mother was bringing up her children on her own was compelled by his mother to go to school. She knew there was no father to take the boy with him to learn ways of earning a living and there were no close relations that she could rely on to do the job for her. She saw a changing world in which school offered her son the best opportunities for making a living wage later on and she sought help and support from the school. The teachers in their turn were welcoming and encouraging. They pursued many of the strategies listed above on a personal level. Yet as a whole, the curriculum did not relate to the young man. The connections were not made for him and he found it hard to see where anything he was learning would be able to be applied to the life he anticipated he would lead after school was finished. He became increasingly resentful towards both mother and school, feeling that neither was giving him what he needed, though when asked he could not articulate what he did need, he had no model and little self-esteem.

The influence of parents' own experience of secondary education is a powerful force. In some parts of the country there are Gypsy Traveller families who have not travelled for many years and there are children in schools today whose parents went right through secondary education. One mother, Mrs J., told me her own tale of her family settling down when they finally got a place on a site. She was sent to school with no great enthusiasm either on her own or her parents' part, but because the 'school board' obliged attendance. They had stopped travelling the roads and taken the relative security of the site place to free themselves from constant harassment. The last thing they wanted was yet more aggravation from the education department and so they went through the motions of sending the children to school. There was little contact between parents and school – the school's attitude at the time seems to have been 'We'll do our best for them when they turn up, but they don't really seem to be very bothered about coming or getting involved when they are here, and often when they come they only cause trouble'.

The parents would take the children out of school for a few days whenever they were needed at home or to go to family events, got impatient when homework was brought home – 'Don't you spend enough time on that school work already?' – and did not consider that anything that went on in school would be remotely of practical use to the children in later life, except maybe a bit of reading. The only time parents and teachers had contact was when there was trouble at school when there would either be an angry confrontation or a tired, resigned acceptance that of course – 'The Gypsies are getting the blame as usual'.

Mrs J. did learn to read but frequently truanted and left school as soon as she could. She married and continued to live on the same site with her husband and then her children. As her own parents had settled and work areas were not provided on the site, they could no longer make a living in the way that they had done before and they started to apply for state benefits. Mrs J. and her husband did the same and she supplemented the income by some calling from door to door to sell goods and tell fortunes and making wreaths for sale at Christmas time. She avoided sending her daughter to school until she was seven – 'What's the point, she's safer with me'. The little girl, Mary, had a severely interrupted education at primary level, she was probably more out of school than in, but was extremely bright and learned to read quickly and easily. Mary, did transfer to the secondary school, but again her absences were frequent and extended. When she was in school she found it very difficult to join any social group because she was so often away. No one at home, parents or grandparents believed there was anything to be gained from school – 'Look at me, what good did it do me?' said her mother.

The school, transformed since Mrs J.'s time there, made every effort to include and integrate Mary but the family attitude was the more dominant and her attendance became increasingly fragmented. The frustration of Mary's disaffection was compounded by the fact that during the periods that she was given home tuition on a one to one basis on the school premises to try to re-establish her in school, she was plainly intellectually stimulated by the academic work which she did, keen to learn and enquire. Now at home she helps to look after the younger children and appears bored most of the time.

What is there to be drawn out from all these stories? In whose interest is it that children attend secondary school in these kinds of circumstances? What are they attending for? What kind of school would work for them and make them feel integrated and fulfilled? There was a time in the early 1980s when I worked as a teacher not only with children from Gypsy and other Traveller families, but also with groups of unemployed school leavers participating in various training schemes. At that moment the particular acronym used to describe the teenagers was YUPs (Young Unemployed People). One group of the YUPs I had was made up of young men of sixteen and seventeen (none of them Travellers), who felt themselves to be failures. They were not fully literate, they had no paper qualifications, they had come out from a tunnel of eleven years of schooling and had no idea of what they might do, no prospect of employment, no sense of value in any of the skills which they did possess. Their self-esteem was non-existent. I ran a session about aspirations. We projected ten years into the future and discussed how we would like to find ourselves then, what we would like to be doing. Apart from one or two rock star and millionaire fantasies the overwhelming majority were remarkably similar to one another. What they all wanted in ten years time essentially was to be married, have a couple of children, have their own homes and work for themselves.

Out of interest I engineered a similar discussion with a small group of Gypsy Traveller young men of a similar age with whom I was also working at the time. None of them had spent more than a few weeks in school in their lives mainly due to the frequent movement of their families. Spending one summer in the area where I was working they had asked for some help with reading so that they could cope with the Highway Code and the road signs for taking their driving tests. Their answers were exactly the same – marriage, children, their own home and self-employment. The difference was that for the young Gypsy Travellers it was more of a prediction than an aspiration, their world was so much more structured despite its instabilities. They all felt fairly confident that that was how it was going to be – indeed they were already on their way. One or two had already bought their own trailers and they had worked, with their fathers in the family economic unit since they were several years younger. Unemployment was not a familiar concept to them in the devastating way it can be for others. They were well aware that mobility and being identified as a Gypsy Traveller would probably preclude them from most opportunities for waged jobs even if they wanted them, and they were accustomed to seeking work opportunities wherever possible. They felt no stigma about not being able to read well – they coped, they asked for help, they seized chances to improve their skills whenever they presented themselves.

This is not to romanticise the Gypsy Traveller group. Their lives were hard, they were not wealthy, they were often exploited and often picked up by the police on suspicion. They faced eviction and hostility constantly, they sometimes broke the law to get by. Observing the two groups I knew who would deal with the adult society they all faced with more confidence. That family support was crucial to the Traveller boys and gave them a structure to identify with was obvious. The YUPs did not enjoy the same family support and neither their families nor their schools had given them the capability of utilising those skills which they had in order to forge an identity for themselves. Neither had they helped them to be aware of the connections between what was learned in school and the opportunities in the world outside. For the Gypsy Traveller boys to have had a similar school experience to their non-Gypsy contemporaries would I am convinced have only alienated them further from the society that sought to contain them. When teachers work now to encourage more Gypsy Traveller children to enrol in secondary school, to increase numbers and improve attendance statistics, the quality of the experience they will have has to be kept at the centre of attention.

Several teachers of Travellers report that increased enrolment of Gypsy Travellers in secondary schools is followed by a greater number of exclusions. Pupils, not finding an environment which offers them anything they can identify with or value, behave in ways which lead to their rejection by the system. A system which they had no wish to engage with in the first place.

There have been enormous changes and upheavals in the education system since the mid 1980s. Schools that are only using some of the positive strategies listed earlier in this chapter will be improving the quality of education offered not only to the Traveller children, but to every child on the roll. It almost goes without saying that schools which do not foster those positive attitudes and actions will still be only likely to alienate their students. It is possible to look around now and see examples of Gypsy Traveller children who have gone right through secondary school, been stimulated by the experience and have succeeded in academic terms. The young woman aiming to be a solicitor is just one. Her parents are supporting her and allowing her to apply to university, moving on from the traditional protective attitude. Gypsy and Traveller cultures are changing and developing as each generation experiences and responds to the developments and changes in the society that surrounds it. Every family, with its own particular circumstances, adapts at its own pace and in its own way, resisting or embracing the changes as they come. Ken Lee, a Romani academic, tells of families who travelled to Australia for easier access to education:

> Some Romanies emigrated from England *precisely* so their children could attend school without harassment.... I know of several instances of Romani parents who sedentarised in Australia only within the last twenty years; some have children who are now graduates of Australian universities. (Lee 1997, p.77)

There can be no generalisations. No part of society nor any culture is ever static and the developments can never be isolated within a culture All change happens in the context of and in relation to every other change in the environment. The patterns of society can be seen as the constantly shifting images in a kaleidoscope, though never with the symmetry of those patterns.

Some Gypsy Traveller parents resist the idea of their children having a wider range of work opportunities through participation in formal education. They see it as part of an assimilation programme by the state and fear the weakening of their extended family networks of support. They see potential harm to the economic base as well as the social base of the family if children move away into other independent fields of work. This possibility can paradoxically seem the more disturbing to families who see ever increasing restrictions on their ability to make their livings in the ways they have been used to and see traditional ways under threat from all sides. There are tight regulations about registering lorries to carry goods, difficult to fulfil without a permanent address. There is an obligation to hold a licence to carry waste materials and a decline in the opportunities to collect and deal in scrap metal. Nomadism itself, and with it the flexibility to move to new work areas as opportunities and demands appear, has been increasingly made more difficult by government policy, particularly with the criminalisation of illegal camping and the repeal of the Caravan Sites Act in the Criminal Justice and Public Order Act (1994), despite the fact that there are insufficient legal site places available.

Yet this is nothing new. Gypsy and other Traveller families have had to deal with shifting economic circumstances throughout the century. George Gmelch writing about Irish Travellers in the period between 1945 and 1960 says:

> The demand for the small household goods Travellers peddled door to door also declined as improved transportation gave country people easier access to shops in provincial towns.... Moreover, just as plastics and enamelware replaced the demand for handmade tinware, other inexpensive mass produced articles reduced the demand for the other handmade crafts the Travellers peddled.... Within a fifteen year period the major trades and services Tinkers performed had become virtually obsolete. The direct causes for their obsolescence – mass production of consumer goods, the widespread introduction of agricultural machinery, improved public transportation, and increased use of the automobile – were external factors over which the itinerant community had no control. (Gmelch 1985, p.45)

Thomas Acton describes the same process taking place in England:

> Mass production made many of the occupations of the Gypsies in the nineteenth century obsolete, from making clothes pegs to making carpet beaters... and towns were large enough to support any number of shops to sell them.... With urbanisation and industrialisation there has been a steady shift in occupations away from small scale trading in new goods and repair services with large numbers of the general public to trade in salvage and construction work, in which there are fewer individual transactions, each worth more.... The modern trades of Gypsies tend to be carried out far more by men than by women. (Acton 1974, p.44)

The shift from horses and wagons to motorised transport during the 1950s and 1960s was also a major cultural if not so much of an economic upheaval. Thomas Acton again:

> Motorisation destroyed a potent range of symbols – in particular, the horse drawn wagon which was still used by only 6% of the families in the 1965 census... much loved horses are now a luxury, while other, previously undreamt of luxuries, electric light, refrigerators, gas cooking, are available in modern trailers: the texture of life has been changed.... The major economic effect of motorisation was, I think, to mask the growing shortage of stopping places: they no longer had to

be at ten mile intervals because a family could travel a hundred miles in a day – and then, using lorries, work over a much wider area, perhaps staying longer in one place to do so. Motorisation, thus economically speaking, propped up traditional Gypsy attitudes and working methods, but as a change in style, I have no doubt that it helped to create a profound feeling among Gypsies that the times were changing, as indeed they are…. (Acton 1974, pp.46 and 47)

The disappearance of the horse-drawn wagon, so much a part of the stereotype of the non-Travellers' image of the Gypsy served only to help ensure that the coming generations of Gypsy Travellers would continue to be rejected by the sedentary population. There was a new rationalisation of hostility – these motorised itinerant workers could not be the 'real' Gypsies whose image had been built up and maintained by layer upon layer of literary fiction. Even now, when many non-Travellers are more accurately informed, there remains a certain regret that the Gypsy Traveller cannot somehow be preserved at an imagined ideal moment sometime after the turn of the century. I suggest that the books which reproduce old photographs of Appleby Fair are popular among non-Travellers for this reason. They are bought and treasured by some Gypsy Travellers too, holding on to fragments of disappearing times. I prefer to confront the realities of the present and the challenge presented by Bibi Anisha:

> The image of what Gypsies and their problems really are, is perpetuated by outsiders who have every interest in preserving their own concepts and cliches and who are always ready to wave the flag of 'acculturation' as if obtaining a better life compromised Romani distinctiveness. This acts as a barrier to development…. This is a false option…. Being integrated into society WITHOUT BEING ASSIMILATED can only provide more strength to affirm our true and human values. The majority population is not 'accultured' because they have a bathroom, electricity, medical care and universities. (Anisha 1997, p.12)

There are all kinds of motivations at work among both Gypsy Travellers and non-Travellers, many social, cultural and economic factors, which are bringing pressures to bear on to the current generation of Gypsy Traveller teenagers. The pervasive influence of television, advertising and recorded music all play their part. It is a time when the young people's sense of themselves in relation to their families and the wider society must be hard to grasp. The place, the influence and the value of school in the equation is not easy to identify.

Máirín Kenny has recently published her research on the experience of Irish Traveller children attending Junior Training Centres (JTC), a form of segregated second level education provision in Ireland. The JTCs were originally set up as almost no Irish Traveller children were moving on to mainstream secondary schooling, yet they did not seem to be achieving their aims. Kenny studies the apparent mismatch between Traveller aspirations and performance in relation to school through detailed observation and analysis of the child/teacher relationship in the classroom (Kenny 1997).

She demonstrates that though the pupils stated that they wished to achieve literacy, nevertheless they consistently resisted the teachers' and school agenda, seeking to and succeeding in controlling the level of work presented to them, which could only lessen their achievements. They 'succeeded in failing'. Kenny describes a complex set of interactions, where a sense of group identity, a consciousness of victimage and enforced dependency lead to resistance and a refusal to accept the sedentary agenda. Often this appeared only to be to their own disadvantage, but occasionally there were moments when the resistance was emancipatory and the children were able to affirm themselves in a positive way.

In secondary schools in England it is possible to see Gypsy Traveller pupils struggling to reconcile various models presented and demands made by schools and family which will enable them to find their own way.

In some ways the issues are different for the boys and the girls. In the earlier part of the century the women in the Gypsy Traveller family had a strong economic role to play. In many families the men made craft and other useful objects which the women would hawk round the doors and sell. On the back of a sale there was often an opportunity for fortune telling. As economically viable work shifted to the heavier jobs of building, demolition, scrap collecting and tarmacking, the men undertook this work and the women were in many cases increasingly confined to domestic and child-rearing roles within the trailer and its immediate surround.

From the perspective of my own culture, which places the highest priority in the raising of children on enabling them to develop to the fullest extent of their individual potential, it is depressing to see many teenage Gypsy Traveller girls held back from this by the expectation that their family responsibility will have a higher priority than their individual development. It is difficult in some cases to separate the several influences of cultural values, economic practicalities and sexism. Many teachers, like myself, find it a sensitive issue to discuss as in a way we present models of what integration or assimilation might mean and it is hard to know the precise motivations when parents reject secondary education for their daughters.

Theresa Griffiths in the report of a Save the Children project also struggles with this:

> One aspect of Traveller culture which I have found very difficult to accept is their expectations for their daughters. In some families it is changing slowly with some of the girls staying on at school and with others undertaking paid work, even if this is only until they get married. Some young women, I think, are exploited by the work they do around the home, even though they are given gifts of jewellery and clothes. Many of the young women expect little better than this on

terms of career and personal development. I can concede that I have no
right to interfere in the lifestyle of another community, but it is
depressing to see so much potential wasted. (Arnold *et al.* 1992, p.22)

When I had the parallel discussions about aspirations with the YUPs and the
Gypsy Traveller boys I also asked some of the teenage Gypsy Traveller girls the
same questions to see if there was any notable gender difference. Some of the
replies were the same – marriage, home, family – but several of the teenage girls
expressed wishes for other careers. One wanted to be a fashion designer, one a
journalist, though they were given as wishes without any belief that there was
any possibility of their realisation. One girl said she wanted to travel! – which
seemed strange at first coming from a young woman within a mobile Gypsy
Traveller group. On further enquiry she explained that she wanted to go to other
places in the world, to see other people independently outside the structured
movement of her own family group, but added that she knew she would never
be allowed.

Bibi Anisha reminds us of the differences in cultural perspectives pointing
out that the roots of Gypsy Traveller culture are Eastern and that it is a distortion
to impose Western values:

It is true that the role and place of the Romni (Gypsy woman) which
is directed INWARDS to her society, in the sense that she is able to
give, maintain and bring up life, is essential; whereas men as the
material support look OUTWARDS from their society. It is normal
for a Gypsy woman to DELIBERATELY love and prefer her own
role. Wherever there has been an attempt to create equity there is
always the impression of being present at a 'de-culturisation' of
sexuality and its various riches. It seems impossible to us to assume
both functions and to fulfil at the same time your own destiny. So we
argue 'Justice' rather than 'equity'. Furthermore it is certain that
Roma and women of nomadic origin generally enjoy great
economic autonomy.

It is true that for Gypsy women commitments beyond the family
are often only possible after they assume their role as wife and
mother. It is common that for wider development she has to reach
the age of maturity. This seems to be right for how can a young
woman, who knows little of life, pain and problems, give an
informed opinion on the important things in life and the future of
Gypsies. Although they lack experience the young ones have more
energy and the desire for change. Nevertheless, it seems to us that
only after the age of passions, deep joys and the pain of heartbreak
has been set aside can the silence and serenity necessary for true
wisdom be created. (Anisha 1997, pp.16–17)

For young Gypsy Traveller men the challenge to create an identity for themselves as individuals and as members of their families and community is different. They have always had a greater autonomy in their movements. For them in the 1990s it is the decline in the work opportunities mainly followed by their fathers and the greater difficulties in maintaining a nomadic habit of life to find work which they have to face.

Their community has always been adaptable and resourceful, picking up new skills to earn a living as conditions have demanded. I believe that many of the skills that would be increasingly useful to them today are to be found and learned in our schools. For the young people to take advantage of them, parents must give the children the support to enter the schools with confidence, to have a stake in and take ownership of the educational process for themselves. I suggest that they should not avoid it as a danger or an irrelevance, or by resistance render it ineffectual as the young Irish Travellers seemed to be doing (Kenny 1997), but by engaging with it create the relevance that they need.

The children cannot easily do it on their own, nor if they are pulled in different directions by teachers and parents. They need a mutual understanding between the two and support from both if they are to be enabled to take charge of their own learning in a positive way. Peer pressure inevitably also plays its part. In a recently published collection of interviews with families on a site in Wakefield the following two extracts epitomise the conflicting pressures and attitudes facing young Gypsy Travellers today.

The first is spoken by a mother of her children:

> They're going to learn, not to be ignorant of the world. They're going to see both ways of life, not just the Gypsy's. My daughter's at school. My husband wants her to leave. She's learnt to read and write and use computers and now he wants her to learn our way of life. He wants her to learn to clean and to look after children. She gets on at school and mixes with gaujes and then our girls don't mix with her. They say she's a gauje. I want her to stay at school. I want her to have a different way of life from cooking and bringing up children. It's important to learn about the world outside the caravan site. I want my daughter to learn our way of life. She's learnt to read and write and use computers and is she going to give that up to learn to clean and bring up children? But I have to fight for her to stay on. (Daley and Henderson 1998, p.60)

The second is spoken by a teenage girl:

> I'm like my mum, people come to me to sort things out. I like mixing with people. Wherever we moved to my mother would book us into the nearest school... so we were always meeting new children. I can read and write and I've been teaching others how to spell their names and to count. Classes are the best thing and I got a Head Teacher's commendation last year. I'd love to be a lawyer. I'd have to go to university. I can only go to school odd days now because I want to help

my mother. But Mrs T. from the Education Service is going to bring me work to do here so I don't fall behind. I can work in the shed or in my brother's trailer and that way I'll keep up. Most Traveller girls finish school at thirteen or fourteen. I know one girl here who stayed all the way to sixteen but you are expected to be at home after thirteen and to help out with the cleaning and the other children. People don't mind us going to school to learn to read and write but then we have to learn the Travellers' way. Other kids on the site call us 'school girls'. Then when you are at school sometimes people at school don't see us for who we are, just that we're Gypsies. It means I'm good at arguing and standing up for myself. (Daley and Henderson 1998, p.68)

For some parents schools can be, consciously or unconsciously, a symbol of the intention of the state to assimilate by enforcing a conformity and promoting a set of alien values. Seeing them reject secondary schools for their children is to revisit the issue of relative power. Their children will be given no chance to benefit from what secondary education can give them to compensate for the decreasing opportunities within the traditional family economy and create new ways of working. Those parents who allow and help their children to get all they can from formal education in addition to their family education will enable them to shape not only their own lives but also to ensure the survival of their culture. Strengthening their own culture will enable them also to have a greater impact on the wider society which currently dominates and often degrades them.

It is hard for Gypsy Traveller children today to assert their own identities in secondary schools and further education because there are so few of them there. They can feel vulnerable and often have little confidence that their culture will be respected. Sometimes their distinctiveness is seen as disrupting, the causes of their alienation are not explored or understood. Secondary schools have an enormous task to respond to the children's needs and create an open environment for them which respects their cultural values, helps them to develop their self-esteem and make the most of their opportunities. Schools have to be ready for the children and the parents who put their trust in them if they are not to reinforce the negative expectations. Teachers in schools have to inform themselves and employ the positive strategies that the best already have in place.

The OFSTED Report states: 'The number of Travelling young people who have access to and take advantage of post school vocational training and further and higher education is worryingly small' (OFSTED 1996, p.8).

I agree with this statement, but I also believe that the numbers are higher than the statistics indicate. The social climate in the past has determined that many of those who have taken formal educational opportunities have hidden their identities in order to achieve the work placements that they have sought and in doing so have only confirmed others' fears of assimilation. The Gypsy

Traveller woman who told me of her own determination to learn in school after the Second World War was both proud of her heritage and of the educational opportunities she had in turn given to her own three children:

> I did the best I could for them – I didn't always have money – I mean we had hardships my husband and I, but I made sure they were at school, talked to the teachers, all the things you've got to do. I helped them with their homework and you know they didn't have private schools or anything, they did it all by themselves. I used to persevere and we all worked together – the husband and the wife – and the parents worked with the teachers. You see when the child comes home complaining you don't go up to school and blame the teacher, you see the teacher and have a word with her. (Kiddle 1997, interview transcript)

Those three children have remained settled and one is now a teacher, one a sales representative and one a technician in a university. They do not speak of their heritage and would not appear in the statistics. Similarly I know a young woman who spent a year doing a part-time course at a further education college, deliberately keeping her identity as a Gypsy Traveller hidden, fearful that she would only meet hostility and discrimination if it were known. She completed the course, living in a trailer on the roadside, but giving a false address and avoiding any possibility of her new friends meeting her family. It is a terrible indictment of sedentary society that she felt she had to 'pass' in this way, deny herself, if she was to have an ordinary college experience. Because she is white and able to hide herself if she feels this is her best option, the college remains unaware of her concerns and her heritage. So they are not in a position to take any action to make sure that any fears she might have had would be groundless.

It is difficult to know the best way to deal with such situations and hard to advise someone to declare themselves and risk facing prejudice so that it may be challenged and addressed. It demonstrates the need for all educational institutions to have a strong anti-racist ethos and an intercultural base to the curriculum whatever cultures they perceive their intake to represent.

A small, but growing number of Travellers have come through the state education system and returned to work within it despite distressing and alienating experiences, taking pride in their own heritage and concerned to ease the way for others. One of them, Willie Reid, a Scottish Traveller, described his own school experience to an education conference when he was a university student. He spoke of a dreadful time when he lost all confidence: 'It wasn't simply that I felt strongly that I didn't share the same occupational aspirations and educational expectations of the majority, it was because I felt trapped in a hostile, threatening and unwelcome environment' (Reid 1993, p.21).

He spoke of rejection by other children, of institutional rejection and of teachers who had made up their minds in advance that the Traveller children would be failures. He stayed because he had to: 'The reason that I had a full secondary school education was because the Authorities gave my mother a simple ultimatum: 'Put them to school or we'll put them in a home.' We learnt in fear'. (ibid., p.22).

Despite this negative school experience a love of learning took him on to university. At the conference he listed the qualities that he felt demonstrated good practice in education professionals:

    – professionals – well informed – well organised

    – recognise our distinctiveness and recognise our ethnicity

YET

    – know Travellers must adapt as they have always done

    – who do not imprison Travellers in the past or by narrow definitions

    – respect Travellers and are respected in return

    – accept individuality – reject stereotypes

    – care, take time, have patience and understanding

    – meet the parents

    – offer advice when needed

    – offer words of encouragement to children

    – gently guide and help children through the school system

    – work day in day out, week in week out, year in year out – against all the odds

    – often disappointed, let down and yet come back and don't give up

    – determined to bring Traveller children to the limitless world of learning so that they can have a bit more freedom, a bit more choice, so that they expect better, whatever they choose to do. (ibid., p.24)

Five years later Willie Reid is still working within the state education system as a specialist Education Welfare Officer with Traveller families and continues to challenge teachers to take a hard look at their own practice. 'What VISION does secondary school offer Gypsy/Travellers for their children?' (Reid 1997a, p.44).

His work, and that of the few other Travellers working openly in state education, is provocative and pioneering, urging a greater involvement of Gypsy/Travellers in state education at all levels.

To work towards a genuine partnership – power sharing – is the only way to make a significant difference for the children. I saw a graphic illustration of this through a number of in-service training sessions which were attended by teachers and parents from another travelling group – the Showpeople from the fairgrounds, whose opportunities for education will be discussed in the next chapter. The teachers and fairground Traveller parents needed to work together to implement a distance-learning strategy for their children during the travelling season. The first two or three training days were attended by many teachers but very few parents. Finally, as the point of the days began to be recognised and the parents understood how important their participation was if the distance-learning system was to succeed for the children, there was a training day when the parents attending outnumbered the teachers. The dynamic of the occasion was immediately changed – the dialogue was more open and direct. The parents knew that their concerns were being heard and discussed and it was possible to sense how constructive the work of the day was when there was a feeling of equal partnership in the interests of the children.

I am optimistic in believing that there are increasing numbers of teachers working with Gypsy and other Traveller families with the qualities described above by Willie Reid and that there are more opportunities for parents, who are willing to work in partnership with them, to become involved. As more and more children become literate and are enabled to go beyond reading and writing to use that literacy as a tool for further self-development on their own terms, I hope that we will get to the stage of the 'critical mass'. A moment when a body of children of this generation of Gypsy Travellers has sufficient confidence in themselves and their capabilities to take all they can from both the state and their family's education and feel no need to assimilate or 'pass' but make choices with a pride in their achievements and their heritage. There is the opportunity for this generation to be given the best of both worlds and for them to begin to feel that belonging to a minority culture is not irreconcilable with being a full member of the larger society. A full education can help not to destroy a minority culture, but to destroy the marginalisation of that culture.

To cope with the disparate influences, the complexities, obstacles and prejudices which they face as they approach adulthood young Gypsy Travellers certainly need all the skills they can get, from wherever they are offered. They also need to be able to make sense of them and see the contexts in which they can be used. They cannot do this on their own. Parents and teachers have to share actively in enabling them to participate and make their education work for them in relevant and realistic ways.

The alternative, the pessimistic view, is a continuing, escalating alienation from sedentary society and a continuing, demoralising marginalisation of a scapegoated minority culture. This prospect is hard to contemplate and leaves little space for the children to build identities for themselves.

CHAPTER SIX

Between Two Worlds

So far this book has focused predominantly on the experience of Gypsy Traveller children and the effects on their education of the relationships between their parents and teachers. I have only made brief references to other travelling groups. I intend to take the next two chapters to examine these effects in relation to the Fairground Travellers, or Showmen.

In 1974 the Bullock Report expressed the view that no child should be expected to leave the language and culture of their home aside as they entered school, nor be obliged to act as if the cultures of school and home should be kept firmly apart. For some groups of Traveller children it must seem as if school and home are two totally separate and different cultures and the fact of travelling itself only exacerbates that sense of distance. Children are regularly expected to move back and forth between the two with too little thought given to how difficult it must be for them. The lives led by children from the fairground community illustrate clearly the conflicting demands made by home and school. Their lives demonstrate vividly how necessary it is for parents and teachers to co-operate and develop partnerships in supporting the children's education if the children are to have any chance of some coherence and continuity in their learning. I chose to look at the fairground community in this chapter and the next because their pattern of travelling determines that the children are not only away for long periods from their base schools, which they attend in the winter months, but also their movements from place to place during their travelling season are frequent and stays at each new location are often short, making school attendance problematic.

Members of the fairground community, who tend to call themselves either Travellers or Showmen, originally come from a variety of different backgrounds. In the late nineteenth century the social reformer George Smith was campaigning to put new legislation through parliament which would, by registering and controlling them, put restrictions on all people who lived in wagons and caravans. The travelling Showpeople recognised that his Movable Dwellings Bill would severely affect all those who lived travelling lives and decided to band together for the first time in order to oppose the Bill. In 1889 they formed the 'Van Dwellers Association', started a campaign fund with membership money, held meetings throughout the country and sent petitions to government. The campaign was successful in defeating the Bill and the Showmen understood how the joint action had protected their community. Their association was renamed the Showmen's Guild and from that time to the present the Guild has developed into an influential national body keeping a close watch on new legislation that might affect its interests and safeguarding the rights of its members. For a few years in the 1920s the then President of the Guild, Pat Collins, also served as a member of parliament. Since the formation of the Showmen's Guild its members have developed a strong identity for themselves as Showmen as distinct from other travelling groups. Entry to the Guild, with its many attendant responsibilities, rights and privileges, is tightly controlled and the Guild has established itself as a firm regulatory body for its members.

The basic pattern of the Showmen's year is also long established. Most families have winter quarters which they return to at the end of each travelling season in October or November. There they remain based for the winter months, maintaining their equipment and preparing for the next year's season, whilst the children return to the schools local to their winter yards. These schools have come to be known as the children's 'base' schools and they generally return to the same schools each year. Most children will remain there until the new travelling season begins sometime before Easter in the following year, though some families may take a holiday in January, the only time they really have an opportunity to do so. Ever changing economic conditions and the recent recessions have meant that some families have extended their travelling season right up to Christmas. Others have travelled abroad to hold fairs in places as far afield as Russia, South Africa, Malaysia and Iceland during the winter months, but for the majority the traditional travelling season still applies.

The new season will begin for most families sometime in March and for the next eight months or so they will be following an individual route from fair to fair staying maybe three or four days, maybe for two or three weeks at each location, but probably with about one week as an average length of stay. Some families will stay within one region, others will travel widely throughout the country. The general run of each family's fairs will be the same each year, as rights to pitches on grounds are retained from year to year, often through several generations. But every year there will also be some changes as grounds are lost to new building developments, the weather affects certain sites or other difficulties arise. Whilst to an outsider the fair gives the impression of being a travelling village, the same families will not necessarily be together from fair to fair. Each family will own its rides or stalls independently and have established rights to place them at particular fair venues which have been built up over a period of time. So each fair constitutes a unique grouping of families. These groupings will shift and change throughout the travelling season.

Even from this brief description it will be clear to see that the school academic year and the Showmen's year are out of step with each other. At the beginning of the school academic year in September, so important to establish friendship groups in a new class, to get to know a new teacher, or to get used to a new school when everyone else is also new, at that time the Showmen's children are still out travelling. In October, when places in secondary schools for the following year must be sought by the parents of children in the final year of primary school, they are still away. By the time the children arrive back in school around mid-November, schools are already beginning to think about end of term events and Christmas activities. The start of the new term in January may see the Traveller children away again on a family holiday, and before Easter they are likely to be on the move again. The under-fives, who might have been due to start school at the beginning of the summer term, will have to wait until nearly Christmas before they get their first taste of school, over six months later than their contemporaries. The whole of the summer term will be lost – the term when the major national exams are taken, the term when most of the liaison and induction procedures take place for transfer to secondary schools. This is the term when subject option choices are made for children at the age of fourteen and careers interviews and guidance are offered. It is in the summer term that many schools offer more opportunities for sports, arrange activities weeks and residential visits, the kind of events which are so important in developing wider skills and improving relationships between the children themselves and their teachers. At every stage of the children's school careers their families' businesses and way of life, which also provide an integral part of their education, prevent them from participating in the mainstream system in the same way as the other children do.

It was not until the mid 1980s that I had any real understanding of all this, even though when joining the theatre company we had bought our first caravan from a Showman's family. Until that time my work with Travelling children had been predominantly with Gypsy and Irish Traveller families. One day someone asked me simply if I worked with the fairground children too. When I replied in the negative the follow up question was – 'Who does that then?' Thinking about it, I didn't know; thinking about it for a little longer it seemed that if our support service were not taking any initiative or any responsibility it was unlikely that any other part of the education service would feel it was within their remit to look at the particular needs of this minority group. I read some case studies about the education of fairground children (Pullin 1985) and decided that we needed to be better informed about the local situation in our area.

I started that summer with the families, visiting every fair I could find as it took place and talked to as many parents as I could. Essentially I was trying to discover how many children were passing through my county during their travelling season, where they had their winter bases, what schools they attended in the winters and what happened about education during the travelling season. As may be imagined I had a wide variety of replies and some suspicion about what I wanted all this information for, no one had expressed much interest in their children's needs before. Eventually I was able to focus on a number of issues that needed to be addressed if the children were to have any educational continuity at all.

Almost all the children, at least up to the age of about thirteen, went to schools in their base areas during the winter. These schools seemed to be really important to the families – 'When we get back to OUR school…'; 'In the winter in MY school…'; 'MY teachers help me in winter to…' – as they were the only places where the children felt they belonged and had any extended opportunity for attendance, even though it might only be for a couple of months. Parents were full of praise for what the schools did during the winter months, though it was plain to see that reintegration each autumn was harder and harder as the children grew older and had fallen further and further behind in their academic work.

As to what happened to the children's formal education during the travelling season, every family had a different story to tell. The only constant was that no one was satisfied with the *status quo*, no one felt that the particular circumstances of their way of life were provided for in the education system. Some children received no schooling during the summer season at all; some occasionally went into other schools for brief periods in the summer where the schools were close to fairground sites and were welcoming to the children. Some parents tried to put their children into different schools every week as they travelled, though no one found this a good experience. Many parents had been sent to school after school themselves and all reported similar experiences that were to become all too familiar of being ignored at the back of the class, given some colouring to do, or being brought to the front to describe life on the fairgrounds. For the majority of them it had been a sad waste of time and opportunity.

Some parents bought commercially produced workbooks for the children themselves and did their best to keep the children going during the summer. No one in my area at that time in 1985 had any work given to them by their winter schools. I discovered later that a tiny minority of families had sent their children to boarding schools or left them back at the base sites with settled relatives during the season to enable a full school attendance. The choice to send a child to boarding school was a difficult one for parents to make. First, this entailed considerable financial strain and sacrifice as there was little help given with fees by local authorities. Second, it meant cutting the child off, not only from parents, but from growing up within the strong cultural base of a show family and the steady, gradual induction into the work of the fairground business. One grandmother talked at length to me about this and how she had come to the decision to send her sons to boarding schools. She herself had wanted to work outside the fairground business but had been given no choice by her father. She wanted her sons to have a choice and she gave it to them through a full education in boarding school. In the event all three of her sons continue to work in the business and have been able to take on work with considerable management responsibilities. This choice was made, however, only by a few parents.

With all this information I made a series of visits to the winter base schools in my area that had been identified by the families and listened to the teachers' perspectives. I was surprised to find that the teachers had absolutely no idea of how important they were to the children and their parents. From their point of view the children arrived back without notice in the second half of the winter term. The teachers had no idea of where they had been or what they had been doing. They did their best for the children while they attended the school, but had little time for assessments to see what standards the children were maintaining or had lost. They conducted a holding operation and within a short time the children were off again without warning for their new season. There seemed to be little useful communication with the parents. As far as most of the schools were concerned at that time, the Showmen's children were with them for such a short time compared to the other children, they did not really consider the children full members of the school. For them to hear that they were appreciated so much by the families as the most significant and consistent educational experience that the children had, was both a revelation and a delight to them. It became a motivating factor on which an improved educational framework for the children could be built.

The identification of this communication gap, which was preventing any educational coherence being possible for the children, gave our service an obvious liaison role. We needed to assess the realistic possibilities for making a connection between the winter and summer, the school and fairground lives of the children in educational terms and try to put a system in place which would give a continuity to their work. A link had to be forged between the Show families and the winter school teachers which would take account both of the children's needs and rights to a full education and the facts of their travelling lives. This link has turned out to be a school-based distance-learning scheme.

To establish the scheme it was necessary to work on a regional rather than a purely local basis as several of the children who travelled within our county during the summer months had their winter bases elsewhere. A co-operative regional network was built up between Traveller Education Services, winter base schools and parents, which was able to learn from and share experience with other regional groupings across the country where parallel developments were taking place. The school-based distance-learning system has been continuing to evolve for over thirteen years now with continuing reviews, evaluation and adjustments from year to year as the long-suffering children have demonstrated by their achievements and attitudes how well the adults have been co-operating on their behalf.

Good practice notes from the experience, which take into account parent, teacher and child perspectives, have been detailed in a pamphlet, *Making Distance Learning Work* (Devon Traveller Education Service 1992). Essentially the central responsibility for the children and their work has to be accepted by the winter base school which has the children on roll and receives the annual capitation allowance for them as for all other children. That school, with support from the TES where necessary, prepares packs of materials, usually separated into two or three week blocks, for the children to take away with them when their travelling season commences. The winter school teachers also complete pages of record books which are given to the children with their distance-learning packs and are kept with their work throughout the summer. The record books indicate the current levels at which the children are working and detail the work sent with them for completion. For their part, the parents are asked to give the school as much notice as possible of leaving dates. Before the travelling season starts, parents and teachers get together for joint training sessions to discuss the work, the logistics of exchanging the packs and other relevant issues. The importance of these developing partnerships between the parents and teachers witnessed in these discussions has been described in the previous chapter and remains crucial to the success of the scheme. In fact as class teachers change from year to year, whilst the parents remain the same, the experienced parents become increasingly significant partners in the training process.

As the children travel, they carry their work with them, working on it either by themselves in their trailers and wagons, with as much support as their parents can give them, or with some tutor support from TES peripatetic staff whenever this can be arranged. At locations where school attendance is possible, the children are able to take in their own work and record books so a continuity can be assured and no time is wasted in unnecessary assessments. The children do, though, still have to contend with continual re-integration and socialising with new classmates. Completed work is returned to the base schools for marking and comment and new packs are sent out. Teachers, from the peripatetic support services or local schools which the children attend as they pass through different areas, support the children either at home on the fairgrounds or in the schools during the travelling season. They add details of their work and comments to the children's record books which then provide the winter school teachers with information about the children's summer achievements on which they can draw when the children return to base at the end of the season.

Those are the bones of the distance-learning scheme which was put into practice and continues to operate, but inevitably the difficulties in making the system work smoothly and effectively have proved to be enormous. Over a period of years it has become apparent that in order for this form of distance learning to be successful six elements are vital:

1   Winter school teachers have to accept their responsibilities fully and be motivated to carry them through. This is a considerable commitment. Class teachers have no initial training for dealing with mobility of this kind and none in preparing materials suitable for

distance learning. There are many implications for both initial and in-service training here.

2   Parents have to accept their responsibilities and work in partnership as necessary to fulfil such responsibilities. This too is a considerable undertaking for parents, who may not be confident in supervising their children's school work in this way and who, like teachers, are engaged in full-time work running their businesses.

3   TES support teachers have to aid school teachers, parents and children in meeting their various commitments and undertake a further liaison role between base schools, other local schools and parents. This kind of extension of responsibility beyond the regular teaching expectation is also rarely covered in teacher training.

4   The distance-learning materials have to be of high quality, targeted to the needs of individual children, and appropriately presented. Yet often those required to make them have little or no training, few resources at their disposal and scant time.

5   The record keeping and work pack exchange systems have to be carefully worked out and kept up to date. Participating partnerships are vital in this respect.

6   The children have to accept their own responsibility for their work and try to make the worlds of the fair and school relevant to each other.

This list is not in any particular order of priority, all elements are essential, and if any one of them does not function as desired, then the system will not work effectively for the child. However, I did put the children as the final point at the climax of the list, because, quite apart from their being the reason for the whole process, their task is the hardest as it raises the central issue beyond that of the management of a distance-learning scheme. What will give them the motivation to make a distance-learning scheme work if they can see no real relationship between the two worlds of school and the fairground? They cannot be expected to engage with the work unless the connections are made.

I have already described the mismatch of the fairground and the academic years and the initial communication gap which I found existed between parents and teachers. Once the distance-learning scheme was in operation teachers and parents did co-operate to keep school work active for the children through the summer months, but there was still it seemed insufficient understanding of the often conflicting expectations and demands that were being made of the children from both sides, that were leaving them (the children) struggling.

Throughout their lives Showpeople gradually acquire the various skills that enable them to run their businesses and continue their way of life. When, by talking to the families on the fairgrounds and having an opportunity to observe their lives, I began to compile a list of the skills they had and areas of knowledge they needed, I realised that it covered a huge range. Some degree of knowledge in all of the following areas is necessary: accountancy, administration, advertising, book-keeping, business management, carpentry, design, diplomacy, driving, electrics, electronics, engineering, law, mechanics, painting, public relations, sign writing, welding… I am sure this list is not complete but it does indicate the range of skills that Showmen and women build up over their lives. As with other groups of Travellers, they feel strongly that it is their responsibility to pass these skills on to their children, to educate them for life in the fairground business.

As the children grow older they are gradually introduced to the various aspects of the business, taking on increasing responsibilities as they are considered ready for them. So teenage boys and girls can begin to have adult responsibilities during the travelling season and take full part in the decisions made by the family about their business. Coming back into school in November, being treated like children again in class, not being able to speak with adults on the same kind of equal terms, having no real responsibility, having lost their place in the social groupings of the class, and probably being made to feel inadequate because in academic work they will most likely have fallen behind their peer group, all this can be dreadful for the teenager. In those circumstances it is quite likely that they will seek to avoid school or alternatively make life dreadful for their teachers too.

Many teachers are not aware of the responsibilities, experience and skills that the Fairground Traveller children are acquiring during their travelling season and so fail to build on those strengths and that knowledge within the school. Similarly parents, who fail to provide their children with reasonable time, working conditions and encouragement to keep up with school work during the summer, may do so because they do not see the relevance of some school curriculum subjects. Yet, whilst some of the skills that the Showmen pass on to their children are beyond any that the school curriculum has time or space to offer, many are not. The practical context in which children learn various skills on the fairground can often easily bring an extra dimension or another perspective into national curriculum subjects. Developing their skills on the fairgrounds, could in many cases extend into practice theoretical knowledge (of basic mechanics for instance) learned in school. Many of the courses on offer in secondary schools today – in communication skills, in child development, in leisure and tourism, business studies, health and safety, food hygiene – Showpeople would find of direct relevance to their children, if they were aware of them.

At the time when, within the TES, we were wondering how best we might promote communication between parents and school based teachers and foster a greater mutual understanding of the two worlds for the sake of the children, new funding possibilities became available. In the mid 1980s the European

Commission had funded research into the educational provision for Gypsies and other Occupational Travellers (defined as Circus, Fairground and Bargee families) across Europe. (A fuller description of European developments is given in a later chapter in this book.) After resolutions were made in 1989 to promote educational opportunities for these groups, budgets became available and a European Federation was established to work with the Circus, Fairground and Bargee families – the European Federation for the Education of the Children of the Occupational Travellers (EFECOT). My service put in a proposal to EFECOT to make a video and, along with other proposals for improving various aspects of distance learning, it was accepted.

The purpose of the video, *Between Two Worlds*, (Devon TES/Marjon TV 1993) was simple enough. It was designed to show a group of Showmen's children, at various stages of secondary education over the period of a year, following them into school, out to the fairgrounds and back to school again. We, as peripatetic support teachers, who in the course of our work spent time like the children in each of the two worlds, wanted both parents and school-based teachers to look into each other's worlds for a while. We wanted them to see the difficulties the children faced as they were obliged to cope with the continual shift from one to another, with all the attendant differences in expectations and demands. We experienced difficulties ourselves in moving from one environment to another and we had far greater control over our experience than the children did. We were concerned that parents and teachers realised that the children could not do it alone and that mixed messages were confusing and destructive. Without the co-operation and support of both their parents and their teachers there was little chance that any educational system set up for the children would be successful.

As we went about the preparations for making the video I was reminded of the story about how one piece of wood provides several heats – as the tree is felled, as the branches are sawn, as the wood is shifted, as smaller logs are split and as the kindling is finally burned. From the very beginning as we discussed the idea with parents and teachers the point of it was being made. Similarly as everyone's lives were disrupted for a while during the filming sessions over the period of a year we had to reinforce the point of it all again and discuss the issues involved so that the most effective shots could be set up. By the time the actual film was there to be viewed all those who had taken any part in it were well aware of the message it was intended to convey.

Being a partner within an EFECOT project had other benefits. We were able to meet colleagues from the Stichting Rijdende School in the Netherlands, an organisation which had been established almost forty years before to create a national system for educating the children from circus and fairground families. Having a smaller geographical area to cover and fewer children within the groups, they had been able to conceive of a national system from the outset and now had in place a highly computerised operation of mobile schools which are stationed on each fairground where at least seven children are present, for the duration of that fair, enabling the children to work full school days with teachers in attendance. The teachers are peripatetic, each working within one region of the country, moving from fair to fair week by week. They do not always see the same children, but the children and parents enjoy the stability of knowing the system and that the mobile schools will be there for them. As in English schemes the children carry with them their own programmes of work and record books from their winter base schools, but during their travelling season can enjoy a level of teacher support and a mobile classroom resource base that we can not approach in England with the current levels of funding.

As the level of peripatetic teacher support that we can provide in England for the fairground children is so much lower than within the Dutch model, and so variable across the country as every TES is different one from another, the quality of the distance-learning materials provided for each child is most important. Whilst our service was engaged in making the video, other project partners in England were taking the opportunity to develop improved distance-learning materials in a range of subject areas across the curriculum. It became evident, however, that teachers could not create independent distance-learning materials in isolation: 'All the elements of the Distance Learning process, from the production and use of work packs to management and support systems, need to be fully integrated and planned as a coherent whole' (EFECOT/A4 1995, p.3).

This was one of the conclusions of a pamphlet later produced to disseminate the experience of the EFECOT distance-learning project. In thinking through the creation, use, follow up and evaluation of the materials the staff of the secondary school involved in this element of the project became concerned with far wider issues of differentiated work, an appropriate curriculum, the presentation of materials, increasing staff awareness of individual needs – a whole staff development process was underway.

There are two distinct strands to the debate that is now widespread among Traveller Education Services in England about distance-learning for Fairground and other Traveller children. One is an interest in developing the systems more and more, to increase the availability of materials, to create banks and databases of distance-learning resources, to involve other travelling groups in the possibilities, to use new technologies to improve communications between students and their base schools. The other is distinctly more cautious and raises concerns about the wider exploitation of distance-learning with Traveller groups without the necessary backup and support. Currently those studying by distance-learning in England, with organisations such as the Open University and the National Extension College, are usually adult, fully literate, already capable independent learners and strongly motivated. Even from firm bases such as these there is a considerable drop-out rate. When we consider distance-learning as a solution to the problem of continuity of learning for

Travelling children, we cannot necessarily rely on any of these bases to provide a foundation on which to build. There is no tradition of distance-learning for children in this country to provide those involved in Traveller education with the results of experience or research findings to be used as guides. Staff of Traveller Education Services have been learning on their feet. 'To learn independently children need to have the necessary resources within themselves; they need a basic level of literacy, self study techniques, a degree of interest and motivation and a belief in themselves as learners' (Holmes and Jordan 1997, p.97).

There is much concern that Traveller children do not go out from their winter base schools equipped to study alone and the support systems are not sufficient to sustain them. There is worry about the quality of materials sent out with the children in situations where many teachers have negligible time to spend on preparing them and few in-service training opportunities to develop their skills in presenting the material in an appropriate way for study by the child alone.

While recognising the benefits that distance-learning can give, the OFSTED report on the education of Travelling children sounds a note of caution:

> Although distance learning cannot be seen as a viable alternative to school, it is providing a successful form of provision in maintaining continuity and giving a support to parents who have the responsibility for providing the education of their children for sessions when they may not be in school owing to travelling. (OFSTED 1996, p.28, para. 77)

There is the possibility that some parents could regard distance-learning as an alternative to school rather than enabling continuity between schools and there is an understanding of this in the position which most providers take – that is that all distance-learning needs to be firmly school based and that the responsibility for the children having access to the full curriculum is rooted in the mainstream schools, who will manage the learning process. Teachers are concerned that some parents without much commitment to school education could otherwise opt for distance-learning in much the same way as some are opting for 'education otherwise' (previously discussed), without a real intention to participate actively on their children's behalf in all that successful distance-learning entails.

There is another anxiety. If distance-learning is developed piecemeal for Traveller children, by Traveller Education Services, without adequate support or record systems, without appropriate resources of staff, time or materials, without relevant teacher training and opportunities for staff development, without a national overview or policy, it may be seen to be offering a second rate, separate education. This goes against the grain for many teachers, the whole thrust of whose work has been to enable Traveller children to have access to mainstream schools and equal opportunities within them. Distance-learning approached without the commitment to a fully professional system is only marginalising Travellers once again.

There is a close relationship in these concerns about distance-learning to the earlier debate in Traveller Education about the use of mobile teaching units for Gypsy Traveller children. Whilst there have been many good reasons for deploying the mobiles, providing a bridge into school, allowing time for fears to be overcome, offering some contact for highly mobile children and so on, there has always been the contingent anxiety that the mobiles would keep the children out of school and deny them their entitlement. The use of distance-learning as a strategy for educational continuity for Showmen's children, where the high level of mobility that their way of life and business demands precludes regular school attendance, could be an excellent one. This will only be the case if the strategy becomes a proper part of a new flexible 'mainstream' education, with appropriate planning, funding and provision.

When we are considering a professional approach to open and distance-learning it is interesting to read material coming from Australia. Tracy Smith, Education Representative of the Romani Association of Australia, writes about the Romani Gypsy people in Australia. There appears to be much less prejudice and denial of access to education and accommodation to Romani people in Australia than in Europe, for most Australian Romanis complete school education and many go on to higher education courses. Many also take advantage of the highly sophisticated distance-learning programmes that are available for all citizens:

> A range of statistics from distance education centres for primary and secondary school children suggest that of the large number of students who use distance education in Australia, approximately half are Travellers.... This term can be taken to include Gypsies, Irish or Scottish Travellers, fairground or circus children, New Age Travellers, the children of itinerant workers and the children of families on long term travelling holidays. (T. Smith 1997, p.21)

The opportunities offered by Australian distance education are totally embedded in the structure of society and the quality of the programmes are not in doubt:

> Distance education is also provided for adult Travellers who are completing their secondary education, studying for trade certificates or working towards a university degree, whether on a part-time or full-time basis. The positive opinion that most Australian Romanies have towards distance education is related to the high quality of the programmes provided throughout Australia. These programmes are flexible, they provide support for children and parents, and the teaching materials are of a standard comparable to the visual, written, audio and interactive programme of face to face education in areas including the arts, learning a second language, English, maths and

> more advanced subjects such as Chemistry, law and economics. In
> most cases, employers regard distance education as equal to face to face
> education. (ibid., p.21)

Within the programmes organised throughout the country for all groups, taking
note of different circumstances, special programmes have been designed to meet
the needs of individual Traveller children, making full use of technology,
providing:

> the regular forms of communication, such as the telephone, radio
> contact, facsimile, E-mail and the internet, available to Travelling
> children; the provision of generators and electronic equipment to
> families where necessary; the study centres in different regions where
> children can drop in whilst travelling to receive additional assistance
> and access to computers.... (ibid., p.22)

In fact Ken Lee, from the Australian university of Newcastle, is concerned that
the acceptance of Romanis in Australia, the lack of an oppression to resist, could
have a dulling effect on cultural identity. (Lee 1997)

Patrick Danaher argues a different point from his considerable research with
others into the use of distance-learning by Showmen's families travelling with
fairs in Queensland. He looks at the concerns felt by some Australians that
'globalisation' in economic and technological terms may mean that the culture
and identity of Australia itself may be overcome and subsumed by the
dominance of other countries particularly the USA. But by looking at the very
particular and local situation of the travelling Showmen in Queensland he
suggests that in fact the education programmes put in place for them are having
quite another effect. He describes a programme which enables:

> the show children to be socialised simultaneously into the distinctive
> cultural traditions of show life, and to receive a continuous formal
> education. This is due largely to the teachers becoming 'itinerant' and
> travelling with their students for a significant proportion of the school
> year, and of their maintaining regular contact with the Show children
> and their home tutors when the teachers return to Brisbane. (Danaher
> and Wyer 1996, p.100)

This particular programme was agreed by the Queensland government in 1989
and allocated to the Brisbane School of Distance Education to run after
successful lobbying by the Showmen's Guild of Australasia and other interested
Showpeople. A travelling group, confident in its own position within society
and determined to find ways to maintain its cultural identity: 'They have sought
actively not to be marginalised from the educational "mainstream", and indeed
to reshape the contours of that "mainstream" to accommodate more effectively
their particular educational situation. Their voices have been heard, and
received a response' (Danaher 1998, p.184).

The parents have been proactive in getting a system to suit their needs and actively work in partnership with the teachers to ensure its success. The demand by the minority group for their particular circumstances to be taken into account, coupled with the long acceptance and professional nature of distance-learning and the communication facilities offered by the new technologies, has meant that for them globalisation has enabled a maintenance of their cultural identity alongside a formal education which has been forced to be flexible to meet their needs: 'For the show people, globalisation constitutes the processes of breaking down traditional and conventional structures of curriculum and pedagogy, while open learning results from the teachers travelling with the show children on sections of the circuit' (Danaher and Wyer 1996, p.105), and:

> Globalisation is being embraced, but its uses and purposes are being defined by the group rather than the group being dictated to by the forces of globalisation. It is in this way that the itinerant group has identified the potential to perpetuate its culture, rather than being totally subsumed by either the majority national culture or the globalised culture.... Rather than globalisation imposing a uniform curriculum and pedagogy on the group, its members are exploiting globalisation to develop a distinctive program tailored to the particular needs of their itinerant lifestyle. (ibid., p.107)

Danaher and Wyer emphasise the benefits to the show children of being able to have the best of both worlds – the programme being structured to their lifestyle reinforces the cultural identity and the maintenance of a full education allows the children to go easily into the surrounding dominant culture when and if they choose to:

> Our study of the education of the show children indicates that such a minority group has the capacity to refine its own culture within the dominant culture and that this capacity is vital if its future generation is to be able to enter the dominant culture at will and to be able to take from that culture whenever required. (ibid., p.110)

In the English context I talk of the Showmen's children being 'between two worlds' with the various implications that there is a struggle to bestride the gap, a constant shifting from one to another or the possibility of falling into an unformed space in the middle. Danaher and his co-researchers talk of 'border crossing'. They see the potential for an easier movement where a minority group maintains its distinctiveness but can operate within the majority society with an equal capability. They suggest that whilst the stereotype of the travelling group is one of powerlessness and marginalisation due to mobility, the Showpeople, by lobbying for and then using the distance-education programme customised to their lifestyle, have in fact demonstrated considerable power. A power which they hope will equip their children with power in their turn to control their futures.

In Australia distance-learning is already a tried and tested system for school age children in many different circumstances, provoked initially by the need to cope with exceptional distances and isolation. From this base the education providers have been able to make particular programmes for the mobile Showmen's children. In England, however, there are no equivalent government funded national schools of distance-learning. There have been experiments in England with mobile circus schools where the teachers travelled with the children, and at one point there were four such schools operating, but none of these schools are now in existence. I would suggest that this is partly because they were not part of a national educational response to accommodating travelling lifestyles, but *ad hoc* arrangements without the necessary support structures. There are one or two enterprises such as the Open School which seeks to offer distance-learning possibilities to children not attending mainstream schools and the Worldwide Education Service (formerly the PNEU which I had contacted when travelling myself) which mainly caters with correspondence courses for families travelling abroad. Largely though, in England, up to this time most distance-learning has been in an adult context. However, there is no doubt that a fundamental goal of all teachers of school age children is to make their students into independent learners. A greater use of open learning and resource-based learning techniques where children learn to manage their own studies within or outside classrooms would benefit all children.

With a background of such study techniques many Traveller children would be far better equipped to complete distance-learning assignments when they went away each summer, nor would they be marginalised or be given second best by undertaking distance-learning. Children need to be enabled to participate equally in education even whilst travelling.

It is not only Fairground, Circus, Gypsy or other Traveller children who experience interrupted learning. In a Staff Development Pack (O'Hanlon 1995) produced to disseminate further the good practice model developed by one secondary school in England through the EFECOT open and distance-learning project, several other circumstances are highlighted in which children's educational continuity is broken for varying lengths of time. They include ethnic minority children on extended 'homeland' visits, homeless families in bed and breakfast accommodation, chronic sick hospitalised children, carers of sick parents, disaffected pupils, those excluded long term and schoolgirl mothers. Schools and the education system struggle now to offer adequate and appropriate educational provision to children in all these groups. Teachers have little training in this area. A greater commitment on a whole school basis to open learning and the creation of more capable independent learners would certainly benefit all these groups. A greater use of independent learning materials within a classroom would benefit every child.

Beyond this a national recognition of the benefits of a more flexible 'mainstream' would be constructive. In Australia, Danaher *et al.* point to the climate of educational thinking being right at the time to accept the Showpeople's case for their own particular programme: 'the emphasis throughout the 1980s and the early 1990s on the rhetoric of "social justice" and "open learning"' (Danaher 1998, p.50).

In England in the late 1990s with a government with a strong agenda for education and social inclusion the time might also be right for looking at ways of extending the borders of the mainstream.

This is one area in which the new technologies can be used to excellent effect. In the summer of 1997, peripatetic teachers in Devon and children travelling with the fair had their first experience of video-conferencing. Whilst at a fair in Devon, a teenager was able to speak to one of her teachers back at her base school in Norfolk to discuss some new work that had been sent to her. One of the Devon peripatetic support teachers reported on the occasion:

> As I had not seen video conferencing before, I did not know what to expect. I had heard the usual stories about the picture and sound qualities being less than satisfactory…. The sound did seem to 'stop' now and again but this did nothing to detract from the realisation that this was a powerful and versatile form of IT that would positively support Distance Learning…. As a form of Distance Learning support I know it will be essential. Here is a way that the student can feel part of the whole learning experience and will be not only able to communicate with the tutor but also with groups of peers and function as part of that group. The method is sufficiently practical and innovative to immediately focus the student's attention and has to enhance their learning strategies, confidence, self esteem and develop communication skills. It will help to consolidate the targets and allow the pupils to feel that wherever they are there is help from the people who really count and that is their own teachers who set the work. It will also help the teachers focus their attention on their responsibilities not only in developing work but also in essential feedback. (Williams 1997, internal report)

His enthusiasm speaks for itself. In this experiment the Travelling children are not being marginalised or offered less than those back in the classroom. They and their parents and teachers are seeing the possibilities of maintaining a mobile lifestyle, keeping contact with a regular teacher and peer group beyond their own social group on the fairground, with the immediate support and liaison of the peripatetic teacher through the use of technology. These experiments are also providing a practical context in which new technologies can be developed which will be helpful for all children. Feedback this year from the TES teacher in Norfolk who had initiated the video-conferencing was positive. She had seen a noticeable improvement in the student's willingness to engage with her winter school on her return.

EFECOT is also extending distance-learning projects using high tech approaches. The TOPILOT project (To OPtimise the Individual Learning processes of Occupational Travellers) is this year (1998) piloting a system in several European countries in which learning units are given to students on CD-is. The students have CD-i players with them in their trailers and as they complete work on screen it is relayed back to their base schools via a central computer in Belgium for comment and feedback. Following on from this, the 'FLEX' project will seek to move these ideas from CD-i to PC systems.

These experiments are taking place, but still in England they are happening in a piecemeal fashion with no overall policy in place. There is a long way to go before we will be able to offer distance-learning to school-age children with the confidence in quality that the Australians can give. However, there is common agreement on both sides of the world that on their own the materials and the technology are not enough. The support systems that engage tutors, teachers, parents and children in active partnerships through an interlinking set of relationships (parent/child; parent/base school teacher; parent/peripatetic teacher; base school teacher/child; peripatetic teacher/child; base school teacher/peripatetic teacher; etc.) are vital for the learning to take place and for the child's right to an effective full-time education to be honoured.

CHAPTER SEVEN

Who is Asking the Children?

Although this book focuses on adult Traveller/non-Traveller relationships, particularly those between parents and teachers, I am determined that the voices of the children come through where possible. This is particularly important within the series of which this book is a part. Their views are under-represented in writings on education generally, as Danaher confirmed in the literature review for his research into the education programme for Showmen's children in Queensland, Australia: 'Despite recent rhetoric describing schooling as a business, a service industry and/or a set of "quality experiences", relatively little attention has been given to the views of the main consumers of educational services – students' (Danaher 1998, p.132). For this reason this chapter concentrates on a case study of a study skills magazine project, which was designed specifically to enable students to have their say.

Over the last few years, as described in the last chapter, work has been going on to get an effective school-based distance-learning scheme operating for the Showmen's children. It has become increasingly clear how hard it is for the children. Even when they have encouragement and support from their parents and are motivated to do the work themselves, very few are capable independent learners when they come out from their base schools each Easter. This is not confined to the Showmen's children, for often the approaches that many teachers take in delivering the curriculum do not prepare children for studying alone. They are not made familiar in school with the ways of working that they are confronted with when the travelling season begins. They have no developed strategies or learning techniques to use. Often they have no idea where to begin or how to organise their time to cope with the study packs.

The logical next step therefore seemed to be to do some work in the area of study skills to try to ensure that the children were better prepared for what they were expected to do. There were various ways that we could go about this, some had already been tried. Each year teachers would go through the work that had been prepared for them with the children before they left school. The teachers would show how the work had been structured and suggest time scales for the completion of each unit. Some had made schedules and charts for the children to fill in as they worked each day or completed sections of work. Some had prepared notes for the children on the ways to use reference books and libraries.

However, the observations of peripatetic teachers, meeting the children periodically through the summer to support their distance-learning, showed that these initial preparations were not sufficient on their own. Very often the charts were not filled in, directions about how to find the way through the packs had been forgotten leaving the children confused. Sometimes even taped instructions had not been played. The children had not been able to take ownership of their work in any significant way.

An opportunity arose in 1997 for a new partnership with colleagues across the European Union in a further distance-learning project under the EFECOT umbrella. Basic skills were to be the focus of attention, so Devon Traveller Education Service opted to work in the area of study skills for secondary level students in order to have an opportunity to search for ways to improve our practice. We already had a Study Skills Group active in the county – a group of teachers from the TES, the Home Tuition Service and the Hospital Schools Service who met regularly to share experience of working with students who were out of school for a variety of reasons and had to work on their own. This group was seeking to discover areas of common ground in the work in order to collaborate on developing mutually useful strategies. The Study Skills Group became the project partner and had to decide on a specific task to complete within the EFECOT framework.

In considering the approaches that we might take to study skills within the EFECOT project, I thought back to the video, which had been made in an earlier phase of the distance-learning project. I knew that the video had had the primary purpose of improving communications and understanding between the children's parents and teachers. Of course the children had been at the centre of the video and the whole purpose of the adult communication was to serve the best interests of the children, yet the children themselves had not been direct participants. They had been involved as 'actors', playing themselves in their roles throughout the year as 'children between two worlds', but only in so far as to present a real context for their parents and teachers each to view the 'other' world for a while. The children had not been brought into the discussions about the making of the video in any substantive way.

It is tempting and so easy to do this when dealing with a minority or a minority cultural group; to treat the group as 'objects of research' or as a 'problem to be dealt with' and make studies and devise strategies without direct reference to the active voice of the group. The host society and the adult world will inevitably start from their dominant perspective, frame the difficulties from their own point of view, and seek to fit the minority group into their pattern. I could see that the overwhelmingly adult perspective was a factor in the challenges that the children were facing in trying to manage their learning packs when left with them on their own. The teachers were in the main putting the units of work together to satisfy curriculum requirements, differentiating the work to take account of the students' individual reading levels and suggesting study strategies that had been useful in their own experience. Only in a minority of cases were the children actively engaged in the preparation of their distance-learning packs.

Lack of sufficient teacher preparation time led inexorably in this direction, but the hours of teacher time that were put into the preparation of the packs were wasted if the children were in the end unable to relate to them.

The members of the group decided that in the Study Skills Project a fresh approach would be adopted that would start with the children themselves. We would ask for their own feelings about being obliged to work on their own, their opinions about the work they were given, the demands that were made of them by parents and teachers. We would ask what they found were the greatest difficulties they faced and what means they devised to cope with them. With this as a starting point we would be in a position to make a proper assessment of needs which should in turn suggest the appropriate process for finding solutions. It seemed though, if we adopted a questionnaire/interview type approach this would take a long time and might simply lead back to more teacher suggestions. If the present students co-operated in the project and articulated their feelings honestly we wanted those ideas, those coping strategies, to be directly communicated to their peer group for the immediate benefit of shared experience. So often in educational projects teachers get together to share experience and make study visits to learn from each other and those meetings are invaluable for professional development, preventing teacher isolation and preventing the interminable re-invention of the wheel. We all trust that children eventually benefit from the improved practice. Student meetings and exchanges are rarer for obvious logistical and safety reasons and for some of those in the isolated and mobile circumstances we were concerned with, virtually impossible.

Taking all this into account we decided to suggest a magazine, written and illustrated by teenagers who were in the position of having to study alone for at least part of the year. The magazine would be produced particularly for others in similar situations. The teachers in the Study Skills Group would have to coordinate the project to be accountable to EFECOT, and finally make the financial arrangements for a print run and sort out a procedure for distribution, but the content, style and design would be the children's own as far as it could possibly be. Our hopes for the magazine were several – that:

- The teachers would learn by listening to what the young people had to say.
- Those who wanted to contribute would have the chance to speak their minds and express themselves.
- The contributors would also gain from the experience of other contributors.

- Other teenagers who read the magazine would realise they were not so isolated as they perhaps imagined and might pick up some good ideas about coping with study.

- Young people would listen more to their contemporaries than they do to their teachers.

- If successful it might generate a successor magazine, which could widen the contributor network. Possible future contributors could be invited to identify themselves in evaluation sheets to be distributed with the magazine.

- At the very least there would be some new reading material around for the children at the start of their next travelling season.

During the summer of 1997 the teachers in the Study Skills Group talked about the ideas with the children with whom they were each in contact and asked if they would like to contribute in some way. There were all kinds of sensitivities involved and confidentialities to be observed. Many of the children on home tuition had been excluded from school and often their lives at home were difficult and troubled. It had to be made very clear to the children and their parents that the subject of the magazine was to be 'studying alone' – the difficulties would be understood, the coping strategies shared. No one was concerned with the background reasons why the child was having to work alone. These would remain private and would only become apparent if the child chose to include them in their contribution and had parental consent. The teenagers were also given the choice of putting their names to their contributions or remaining anonymous.

The teachers working with the Showmen's children had the advantage of being able to invite participation from those over sixteen, who had left their days of distance-learning packs behind, but who were still accessible, working with their family businesses and watching their younger siblings trying to cope in their turn. These young men and women, some of whom had had distance-learning packs in their travelling season right through their school careers, who had indeed been the pioneers (or guinea pigs as they put it) of our developing system, were able to offer a uniquely valuable perspective from their long-term direct experience.

Some of the comments we collected demonstrated clearly the isolating nature of distance-learning and the importance of the base school taking responsibility for the students in a complete way. No matter how good the distance-learning packs might be, if they were not integrated into the main work in school in a way that the students and staff could appreciate, their value would be diminished.

> I think it was in my third year (year 9) I got really fed up because when we used to go away we used to work as hard as we could but when we got back in school they just didn't bother with us. They said, 'Oh

you're only here for a couple of months so you can draw something on that piece of paper.' I felt that the work I'd been doing all the year was lost. But the next year after I came back in again I did GCSEs and GNVQs and got through. I should have got better grades really. The work was a lot better, I enjoyed it more. For the exams I picked the things I was really interested in. I loved Humanities and I liked the teacher as well… I liked the last couple of years in secondary school more than I did the first years really. I realised what I needed the exams for and what they meant…. It's helped me a lot. I wish I had stayed at school all year, but it's over now. (Devon Consortium Traveller Education Service 1998, p.9)

Virtually everyone who was asked agreed to take part in some way and some were plainly pleased that their opinions were being sought at last. When, on the fairgrounds, the idea was first discussed with groups of children, a torrent of pent up frustrations was released and we were offered a whole catalogue of moans and groans. After this initial blood-letting teenagers talked to teachers individually about the possible contribution they might make and were much more positive and constructive in their attitudes, welcoming the chance to put their point of view, wanting teachers and others to understand how they felt.

The ways in which the children made their contributions differed according to each one's circumstances. Most of the non-Traveller children, who were studying alone because of illness, exclusion from school or some other reason. completed drawings or written work during the course of their support sessions with their home tutors. For home tuition to be effective a relationship of co-operation and trust has to be built between tutor and student, and it was from the basis of those existing relationships that the tutors were able to discuss pieces for the magazine. Even so they were surprised to find that the young people displayed an unprecedented openness when invited to address the issue of what working alone meant for them. The two home tutors taking the lead in the project as members of the Study Skills Group both commented that for several of the students, their contributions represented the best pieces of work that they had produced during their time on home tuition. Neither the tutors nor the children's parents had been fully aware previously of some of the feelings expressed.

> I feel very alone and you want to go to school but you can't. You feel like you are the odd one out and sometimes it makes you sad and it's hard to tell anyone. Your friends wonder why and sometimes they make fun of you but you get used to it. And sometimes you think about when you are older and you wonder if you are going to get a job. I have got used to having a Home Tutor but one day I hope I will get back to school. (ibid., p.1)

> It's like being disabled, you don't feel as normal like most kids of your age. My teacher used to have to walk me in to class and I felt like an

> outsider. When friends and family come around and say, 'How's school?', I used to have to say, 'Fine'. When I am at home watching television when I feel I need to work I can't. It's like a big hole in my school life and every time I try to sew it up the thread keeps snapping and I'm back where I started. I used to have a good friend, but now it feels like he's got to look after me because of my problem. When I watch television programmes like Grange Hill I get really jealous because I feel like I should be going to school like them. You can give hints about how you feel about school but no one really understands. (ibid., p.2)

It was something of a surprise to all of us to find that not one of the participating children enjoyed being out of school. Everyone on home tuition spoke of what they missed in school, particularly friendship and not being able to be part of a group, and indicated a hope to get back there in time.

On the fairgrounds the children made contributions in a variety of ways. Some went away by themselves and came back with a drawing, a story or a puzzle. Others chose to talk on to tape on the understanding that they could then join in editing the transcripts. As the pieces came in they were grouped under generalised headings – how it feels to work on your own; what we'd like to tell teachers; what we miss about school; how hard it is to go back; the difficulties and distractions of working alone; how we cope; keeping going and finding your own talents; don't have regrets; agony aunt letters. It was interesting to see how many of the ideas, attitudes and opinions were common to the children whether they were out of school through exclusion, sickness or travelling. Everyone agreed about how hard it was to go back into school after a period away:

> The worst thing is when you go back to school the work doesn't match up to the work they are doing.... Every teacher is telling you a different thing and you get so fed up that you can't be bothered to go to school. (ibid., p.5)

> The teachers don't explain it enough. They just give it to you and say you've got to do it and you're expected to sit down and have to do it. (ibid., p.5)

> When we go back to school it's quite hard because we don't know what they're doing when we go into a classroom. (ibid., p.5)

One spoke for all about the difficulty of self motivation when working alone with distance-learning packs:

> All you know is that once you've done that work you're going to get another lot sent to you. (ibid., p.3)

The frustration of trying to cope with some packs came through loud and clear:

> The packs weren't put together right – not all the papers were there for the maths. On geography loads of the maps were missed out and we don't have an atlas. (ibid., p.3)

> The troubles I had with French! I had a work pack and a tape, but the tape was never the right one. (ibid., p.3)

> She writes questions but she doesn't explain it. (ibid., p.3)

> The Science they give you – they ask you to do experiments but you can't get hold of the equipment. (ibid., p.3)

> When I had the same work for three years – look, cover, write, check – I said I ain't doing this any more. (ibid., p.3)

The distractions were ever present:

> Working at home is difficult. I have a little brother who is three years old. He wants me to put a video on for him. Or go to the park with him. He likes me to play cars with him. (ibid., p.6)

Yet most of the teenagers were working out their own coping strategies, sometimes using the mutual support of their peer group where possible:

> When the teacher wasn't there I used to limit myself. I'd get my book and I'd say I'll do so much work and then I can read a page of the book. (ibid., p.7)

> That year J was doing the same subjects and it was really helpful working together, because even though we went to two different schools in the winter we had the same sort of work.... When she went away to a different ground, she'd ring up and say, 'How much have you done? – I've done such and such.' That was really good. (ibid., p.7)

> I always wanted to do an hour first thing in the morning. (ibid., p.8)

> I used to wait till we got to quiet places... then I'd go at it all day. (ibid., p.8)

> Well, if you're going to do it you've got to keep doing it a little bit at a time... everybody's got their favourite bit to do – like maths – it's best to leave that till the end. Do the bits you don't like first and then you've got that to look forward to. (ibid., p.8)

> Sometimes I do one page a day. I try and do it myself and if I can't I get it out again and see if I can do it the next day. (ibid., p.8)

When they had problem letters to answer the students could make suggestions directly from their own experience:

> Dear John,
>
> If you want somewhere to work and it's not possible in your house go to your local library or ask your home tutor to take you to a centre. Talk

to your parents and tell them you need to do your homework and you can't do it because you are being interrupted all the time. Make a timetable when to study. Plan difficult things for the morning because your brain is in gear then. Show your timetable to other people and ask them to help you to keep to your times. You need to get your family on your side to help you out. Try to make them understand. (ibid., p.13)

Contributions came in over the summer and in the early autumn a group of teenagers who were attending the same fair agreed to act as an initial editorial group, to choose a title (*Get it Sorted*), give ideas for layout and design and come up with wording for an editorial. During the winter of 1997 and early spring 1998 the final editing and design were completed and a print run had the magazine ready for distribution just before Easter. *Get it Sorted* has been disseminated quite widely in England and copies have gone to other countries in the European Union. The initial reactions have been very positive, but at the time of writing evaluation is still underway. It is possible, however, to reflect on the group's own and other initial reactions to the project.

First there is no doubt that the children were pleased to be asked. It did not seem as if any of them had had the opportunity to participate in such a forum previously. At a European conference (Beyond Reading and Writing) organised by ACERT and Oxford Brookes University during September 1997 on the theme of Travellers and secondary education, several participants were invited to inform others about current European projects. I gave a resume of the intentions of the Study Skills Project on the lines of this chapter. I had hoped to be accompanied by one of the teenagers from the fairground who was involved in the magazine. However, at the last moment she did not quite have the confidence to attend. Colleagues at the conference asked:

- If it would be possible to include contributions from young people in their areas in the current or a future magazine.

- How wide the distribution would be – would they be able to have copies to use with their own groups of teenagers.

These responses gave a welcome validation to our initial intentions, indicating that others too were well aware of the potential benefits of enabling young people to offer each other mutual support.

In November 1997 I gave another short presentation about the project at the EFECOT Congress (In Partnership We Progress) in Blankenberge. This time one of the teenagers from the fairground community did join me. He was attending the Congress with his father, who was making a separate presentation about the Showman's way of life. Alan was able to speak directly about his experience of studying alone to an international group of teachers, administrators and policy makers and did so with great fluency. These were all positive events.

However, it was difficult to maintain for the teenagers the sense that it was really 'their' magazine. Their separation from each other and the timescale that the whole project was obliged to have were such that keeping a momentum going and a sense of ownership for them was problematic. In contrast a school setting would have provided a continuous sense of the process of the making of a magazine. Even though tasks – writing, editing, illustration, design and layout – might be handled by separate groups within a class, the whole class would be aware of and be able to discuss the various stages of production. There would be a much shorter timescale and a continuing engagement.

That we could not provide. The best we were able to do was to keep revisiting the individual contributors, to consult on the presentation of their contribution, to inform them of the stage that had been reached and to ask for their opinions on design ideas and layouts. It was more difficult for the home tutors than for the peripatetic teachers of the Show children. Some of the children on home tuition moved into other areas or circumstances during the course of the project and could no longer be involved. Their individual situations had none of the stability which the fairground community offered despite the frequent travelling, and in the end the range of children being tutored at home was not fully represented. We were able to bring together small groups of Show children as they attended particular fairs so that they could take part in editorial discussions. A few generated design ideas and were involved with computer page layouts. There was a delay whilst we waited for budget authorisation for printing. Inevitably the teachers in the Study Skills Group had to provide the continuity and the contacts and maintain the level of interest and motivation to see the project through. Certainly the periodic discussion of the contents, all centring on the issue of studying alone, was helpful to both teachers and students.

When the magazine was finally produced the contributors were able to take ownership of it once again, and all those who we could contact were delighted with it. Sadly, one or two on home tuition had moved on and could not be traced. There was an opportunity for one of the home tutors from the Study Skills Group to bring two or three of the teenagers who had contributed to the magazine to meet a few of the Show children when the fair came into their town. An afternoon visit was arranged when the mobile classroom, used by the TES peripatetic teachers to support the fairground children with their distance-learning, would be at the fair. This would provide a suitable venue for the children to meet and talk about the magazine. However, although the home-tutored children came with their tutor by car to the fairground (and this the tutor considered a success in itself), they could not be persuaded to meet the teenagers from the fair. They spoke to the TES teacher, but were unable/unwilling to talk with their peer group. It was difficult for them, preoccupied with their own isolation, to make connections or relationships with those in other circumstances. It is hoped that the magazine idea may in time help the children to relate their own thoughts and opinions to those of others and that they can begin to make connections.

I have described this Study Skills magazine project at some length, not because it is unique or particularly startling or innovative, but because I believe it exemplifies many of the difficulties for Travelling children and others with interrupted educations. Increasingly in schools up and down the country children have opportunities today to be direct participants in the debate about their education. Circle time activities allow their individual voices to be heard; school rules and bullying policies are arrived at by debate and consensus; children are to a much larger extent involved now in school councils, on committees and in mediation projects; magazines such as I have described and school newspapers are produced on a regular basis. But those children who are not regularly or fully part of school life are never completely part of the group and are therefore not able to benefit from the changes which are taking place as regards children's involvement in the educational process. The difficulties of returning, of coming back in, even to a familiar school, is a recurring theme of the teenage writers. Every class, every school has its own dynamic with which it is not easy to re-integrate.

Whilst it is hard to keep fitting in to mainstream school life, at the same time there seems to be little understanding of the need to give an importance to the special set of dynamics that those with interrupted educations have in their lives. Probably precisely because these children are comparatively few in number, because they are isolated, because they do not have a group power in their own situations to influence practice or effect change, because they do not have the opportunities to make themselves heard except in close personal situations where their voices can be perceived as disruptive. They have to rely on teachers and parents to act for them. The magazine project, if successful, will be a tiny step on their road to empowerment.

The challenge to teachers is to continue to search for practical ways in which this group of children can make their voices heard. The issue for teacher training is to increase sensitivity to those in these situations. The project described, arising out of distance-learning and the necessity at times to work at home alone, has involved Travelling children from the fairground community, but the need to enable the children to be active in the debate about themselves, their education and their identities is common to every Traveller group.

CHAPTER EIGHT

Speaking for Themselves

It is not only Gypsy Traveller, Fairground and other Traveller *children* who have had few opportunities to speak for themselves, the voice of the *adult* Gypsy Traveller has rarely been heard by the non-Gypsy world. How much of what non-Gypsies know, think they know or believe about Gypsy Travellers has come to them directly from the people belonging to the group? Very little I suspect. I imagine that my own childhood experience was similar to that of many other town dwellers of my generation. Occasionally Gypsy Traveller women came to our door selling paper flowers and white heather, but beyond that I saw and knew nothing of them. For those who lived in the country areas it may have been different. My attitudes and impressions were largely formed through literature. I have clear memories of several books with Gypsy characters which I read as a child; none of them were written by Gypsies, though this never crossed my mind at the time. When I first read Dennis Binns' study (Binns 1984) of the role of the Gypsy in children's literature, written whilst he was working as a teacher of Travellers in Manchester, it came as something of a revelation to me. I began to trace the making of the stereotypes that had been in my head before I met, lived and worked with Gypsy and other Traveller families.

Binns looks at the role of the Gypsy in 120 books written for children between 1814 and 1984. He concludes that the various stereotyped images built up over 150 years of children's literature must play a large part in perpetuating the deep anxieties and hostilities that are demonstrated by non-Gypsies towards them:

> A study of children's literature, or any literature, cannot reveal any other group of people so constantly maligned and ill-represented. If an author introduces a Gypsy into his or her story then it is nearly always for a reason other than portraying the Gypsy as a human being living his normal life.... The great majority of writers use Gypsies as a literary device or symbol. If they wish to illustrate their work with a pariah group, a thief, a child stealer, a romantic group, a person with magical powers: they bring in Gypsies. These are very useful devices for the author for explaining away displaced children, robberies, strange events, evil or magical happenings. It is a very convenient device for they could not use any other group of people and still remain credible.

> Gypsies still represent, for authors and readers alike, that unknown
> quantity that can explain away the impossible. (Binns 1984, pp.6–7)

It was only in the 1970s that things began to change with the stories by
Geraldine Kaye ('Nowhere to Stop' etc.), then Olga Sinclair ('Gypsy Girl') and
Rumer Godden ('The Diddakoi'), but even now, over ten years after Binns was
doing his study, the stereotyping still occurs. The lack of accurate information
available on a widescale to the public, the continuing marginalisation of the
Gypsy Traveller in society, through hostile attitudes or repressive legislation,
still renders the character – as scapegoat, as outsider or conversely as an exotic,
romantic figure – useful as a device for moving a plot forward. It was almost
thirty years after the end of the Second World War before the full knowledge of
the suffering and genocide of the Gypsies alongside the Jews in the Holocaust
was brought to public attention (Kenrick and Puxon 1972) and another decade
before these facts were presented in a book for schools (Acton 1981). The
unproven fictions of child stealing by Gypsies were common in children's
literature and are familiar to all, but it is still relatively unknown that a Swiss
charity, Pro Juventute, was taking Gypsy children from their families and
relocating them within the sedentary society right up to 1973:

> In 1926 the eminently respectable Pro Juventute foundation decided,
> in keeping with the theories of eugenics and progress then fashionable,
> that the children of Jenische ('Travellers') should wherever possible be
> resettled, in order to divert them into the mainstream of society; thus
> began a system of taking children away from their parents without
> their consent, changing their names, and placing them in foster homes.
> These institutionalised abductions continued until 1973, by which
> time over 600 children had been forcibly removed. (Fraser 1992,
> p.254)

Gradually more accurately informed representations of Gypsy and Traveller
peoples are being made in factual and fictional writing, but they are still in the
main being made by non-Travellers. Even in song I would suggest that the folk
ballads about life on the road, 'Moving-On Song' and 'The Thirty Foot Trailer',
written not by Gypsy Travellers but by Ewan McColl (McColl 1983), are
probably the most well known.

In his study Binns remarked: 'It is probably safe to say that almost all books
in British schools are written by non-Gypsies and furthermore, the vast majority
of the books are written with non-Gypsy children in mind' (Binns 1984, p.9).

I think this statement is still accurate today. During the 1970s, two Gypsy
Travellers, Gordon Boswell (Boswell 1970) and Manfri Wood (Wood 1973),
and a Scottish Traveller, Betsy Whyte (Whyte 1979) wrote and published their
autobiographies and provided at last and at least for the adult market the
foundation stones on which others could build. In Ireland, Nan Joyce followed
with her autobiography (Joyce 1985). Traveller written stories I believe first
came into British schools with a wide dissemination through an established

publisher in the 1980s, when Duncan Williamson, a Scots Traveller and storyteller, was encouraged and aided by his second wife (a non-Traveller) to put the heritage of his oral culture on to the page (Williamson 1983). There had been several collections of Gypsy folk-tales available for schools before this, but all collected, rewritten or edited by those from outside the culture. As recently as 1995, in an introduction to a collection of poems written by a Traveller Charles Smith, Paul Lincoln, Director of Education for Essex County Council, wrote: 'Traveller children have few role models and see little of their own culture on book shelves to recognise and value its importance' (Smith 1995, p.5).

For my generation the image of the Gypsy, which had been laid down for us by the children's literature we read, was reinforced for us as adults by the work of the folklorists. Many folklorists and others coming into contact with Travelling peoples, observed and heard elements of an oral tradition which they believed was disappearing in a fast changing world increasingly dominated by television and recorded music and sought to preserve that cultural heritage in print, through photography and on tape. The result has been to crystallise those images and perceptions of the traditional Travellers into the dominant stereotype most of us hold today as that of the 'true Gypsy'. Unsurprisingly when we meet Gypsy Travellers today they do not conform to the traditional stereotype and so we think that they cannot be 'the real thing'. We resent the late twentieth-century Gypsy Traveller for not fulfilling our preferred image, for not residing in the sepia zone where none of us would have to confront the acute accommodation and other issues of the present time. It is time that we started to deal in realities rather than fantasies and nostalgia.

> Up to now, Gypsies and Travellers have been *invented* by observers; it is necessary that they be *recognised* for what they are, in all their richness and originality, because co-operation in a spirit of mutual respect is the difficult but crucial precondition for improving their living conditions and achieving mutually enriching coexistence. (Liégeois 1994, p.312)

In Britain literate Gypsy Travellers are beginning to use print media to identify themselves. They are tired of outsiders doing it for them:

> I believe that too much is being written and told of the old ways...the Gypsy community of this country does not spend all its time hunting rabbits or going to Appleby Fair; we don't sit around camp fires all day telling old folk tales while we make pegs or paper flowers. No the truth is, just like everybody else, we are involved with today's modern world.... I fear that if we spend too much time living in the past we shall miss what is really happening today and if we do that, we just entrench ourselves into the stereotypes that many in the non-Gypsy society want us to be. (Smith 1995, p.6)

In examining the relationship that the folklorists have had with Scots Travellers, Willie Reid says: 'As a Gypsy/Traveller myself I am made painfully aware that we have always been defined by outsiders…' (Reid 1997b, p.30).

He asserts that the folklorists have created a nostalgia culture, which enables us to look to the past in comfort, and that they have taken over the Travellers' oral culture and made it more a part of the Scottish heritage than distinctly that of the Gypsy/Traveller. 'In robbing us of our oral culture, researchers have taken oral treasures that have been preserved throughout the centuries. It is time Gypsies/Travellers reclaimed these, re-examined them and built upon the oral tradition' (ibid., p.36).

I believe that as the inheritors of an oral culture, Gypsy Travellers have always been well aware of the potential advantages this gives them in being able to keep outsiders at bay and they remain so. I have referred in an earlier chapter to the research of Donald Braid in which he demonstrates the ways in which the identity of the Traveller and the relationship of Traveller to non-Traveller so often emerges in narrative events conducted by Travellers when non-Travellers are present. A West Country folklorist, Sam Richards, described to me his fieldwork experience in collecting songs from Gypsy Travellers during the early 1980s. When Travellers agreed to sing for him or let themselves be recorded on tape, very often the first song to be offered would be 'The Farmer in Leicester' or a version of it. In this song a young woman is going to market when she is attacked by a highwayman. She is stripped and robbed, but manages to get her foot into the horse's stirrup and escapes taking the highwayman's horse with her. She later finds more money in the saddlebags than was taken from her. The song, with its appreciation of horsemanship, shows how the seemingly vulnerable and weaker party can outwit the stronger. No analogies were ever made explicit to the Traveller/non-Traveller relationship, but the song nearly always made its appearance at the beginning of any Traveller's first recording session with Sam. The ground was in this way being set.

In the late 1970s, after I had moved from London to the West Country and began to work there with Gypsy Traveller families, whom I had not known before, I rarely heard any words of Romani spoken. Sometimes I would be aware that a conversation stopped or was abruptly changed when I entered a trailer to talk to a family. Occasionally I would hear myself or some other visitor referred to in words spoken so softly or quickly that I could not catch them. When I asked about the language I was given generalised evasive answers. As time went on and I came to know families better, I heard Romani words and phrases used more often. At first I thought that I had just not noticed them previously, but it became ever more clear that the language was used more frequently as families were more relaxed in my presence. It was not for me to share, but was no longer hidden from me. Inevitably I came to learn and understand more of the language as it was both used in front of me and has become publicly more available in books, articles and dictionaries in the last few years. For me a defining moment of a relationship with a Gypsy Traveller woman came as we were sitting talking in her trailer one afternoon. Another woman, plainly a non-Gypsy, and a stranger to both of us, came to the trailer door. As she opened the door to speak to the new visitor, the Gypsy Traveller woman asked if I knew who the woman was, using a few words of Romani that she knew I would understand.

Whether they like it or not, much of the secrecy of Romani has been taken from the Gypsy Traveller peoples. Among themselves, in continental Europe, the debate has moved on from whether to write the language down, to trying to reach an agreement on which dialect form should be the basis for a standard Romani. (The outline of this debate can be traced in successive issues of *Interface* magazine.) This debate, however, currently only has meaning for the literate Gypsy Travellers. Up to the present generation in England the majority of Gypsy Travellers have not been literate. Their culture has been passed on within the group, but little has been written down directly by them for others to share and understand. The result has been that they have been defined by others, their oral culture has been taken and written down by outsiders, their image has been manipulated and constantly reshaped for the convenience of the dominant sedentary group. Inevitably the outsider view is shaped by the relationship within which it is formed. To a certain extent the 'inside' group can control the information which is given. The way in which the information is perceived will depend on the attitude and the agenda of the recipient and the circumstances in which it becomes known.

In 1984 the Gypsy Sites Branch of the Department of the Environment published a paper, 'Defining a Gypsy', trying to make some sense of the confusions that local authorities were then facing in fulfilling or avoiding their legal obligations to provide sites for Gypsies under the 1968 Caravan Sites Act. In the introduction the following statement is made:

> The facts in this paper have been obtained from the literature on the subject and from useful conversations with those who are knowledgeable about gypsies. Gypsies are not the best source from whom to get information about themselves as they often say what they think or hope the questioner wants to hear. (Department of the Environment 1984)

This comment takes us straight back once again to the complexities of the interactions between identity and power relationships. Leaving aside for a moment whether the Gypsy Traveller has or could have the power to alter the stereotypes, there is no denying that when they need to, they will use the various stereotypes of themselves, as we all do. Outside the group there can be both advantage and disadvantage in being identified as 'Gypsy'. A Gypsy Traveller woman, calling to the doors to sell lucky charms or tell fortunes, may dress and speak in a way that consciously exaggerates the stereotype she knows that others have in order to attract customers. Conversely a Gypsy Traveller man, looking for building or roofing work, may hide his identity knowing from long experience of prejudice that if he is identified as 'Gypsy' then he will also be perceived as untrustworthy. Such pragmatic alteration of outward image according to circumstances is discussed in-depth by Judith Okely. Okely points out several different ways in which Gypsies may shift their ethnic image in dealing with non-Gypsies, but she says: 'These modes rarely coincide with the Gypsies' own image of ethnic identity' (Okely 1996, p.52).

Somehow, Gypsy Traveller families keep hold of a central sense of themselves, their beliefs and values. The difficulties in doing this are legion. For some, hearing the constant denigration of their culture has led to an extremely poor self-image and a lack of self-esteem. One day in the mid 1980s I was working with a group of teenagers in a small kitchen trailer on an unofficial site at the back of a council refuse tip. At the time we had not been able to get the children to school and I was doing some basic assessment and literacy work whilst we were negotiating for school places. One of the mothers called from her own big trailer for me to come over. I thought I was being offered a cup of tea, but when I entered the trailer, quickly followed by the children, I found a group of parents sitting together listening to a radio phone-in. It was about them. They were camped illegally as there was no official site in the town; the council was thinking about making a site; the local residents were highly antagonistic; the local radio station was making it the issue of the week for the phone-in programme. We all listened for a while and I sat there, the only non-Gypsy, embarrassed and appalled, hearing one after another of my own people spitting abuse, trailing the stereotypes, declaring affection for the 'true Gypsies', but these... speaking so often as if the people were less than human. I watched the children's faces as they tried to come to terms with being so reviled.

I suggested they phoned in to the programme themselves, but none would do it, they asked me to speak on their behalf – 'Tell them we're not like that'. I was not at all happy with this idea, but was finally persuaded to telephone, agreeing only to speak from my own perspective. No one had a mobile phone in those days and I had to drive for two miles to get to a telephone which I could conveniently use. When I got through to the programme and explained why I was ringing I was immediately connected to the presenter and found myself suddenly 'live' on air. I gave factual information about the site issue as I knew it and explained the circumstances in which I had heard the earlier part of the programme. Asked 'What do the Gypsies think?' I could not reply, but only asked the other callers to consider the effects that their words might be having on the Gypsy Traveller children who were listening.

I then had to return to the site to face the parents who had also been listening to what I had to say. I discovered that after my call the presenter had decided to close the topic and had moved on to discuss other issues. We were all pleased about that, but I was disappointed that none of the parents had been willing to speak out themselves. I could not say whether it was an unwillingness to take part in a 'gauje' debate, or a lack of confidence in being able to command the appropriate language in an unfamiliar situation.

However, hearing the depth of the antagonism of some of the callers to the programme it is easy to see why some Gypsy Travellers who have settled in housing with non-Gypsy neighbours have chosen to conceal their identities.

In legal terms, ethnicity has in the past been denied. In making a definition for the 1968 Caravan Sites Act, Gypsies were – 'persons of nomadic habit of life, whatever their race or origin'. It was only in 1988 that a Court of Appeal judgment (CRE v Dutton) confirmed Gypsies as 'a racial group' as defined by the 1976 Race Relations Act.

The ever developing culture and sense of identity of the Gypsy Traveller has been affected at every stage by the surrounding environment. David Smith writes about the negative effects of social pressure on attempts to adapt a traditional decorative art form to the Gypsy Travellers' modernising world. As families moved from highly decorated horse-drawn wagons to lorries and trailers, they began at first to incorporate the old designs:

> For a brief period during the 1950s and 60s the painted motifs of the wagons and carts were applied to the door panels, wings and bodywork of the motors used to tow the newly acquired trailer caravan. Unfortunately when this unique form of decoration was applied to mass produced vehicles it made them quite conspicuous and they were subjected to frequent police checks. As a consequence this form of vehicle embellishment ceased, creating an unusual situation in which a developing folk art form was abruptly halted through the activities of an external agency. (Smith 1997, p.10–11)

There is a parallel to this going on today, as many Traveller families are selling their individualised highly chromed trailers for more conventional models: 'Some Travellers think that the flashy chrome trailers make you stand out too much. They have bought the new German Weippart trailers which are plainer. It is easier to pull on trailer sites with them' (Reilly 1995, p.10).

Despite all this, maybe partly given strength because of the will to resist the constant repression, the Gypsy Travellers' ethnic culture has survived. The sense of pride in their own identity has up to now been largely kept inside, within the cultural group, treasured like the collections of photographs that provide growing family archives and which have a special and significant place for everyone. The outside, the 'gauje' world, has been kept at a distance by a range of strategies, some of which I have described. There could be a parallel drawn with the physical and literal 'inside' and 'outside' of trailer living. The immaculate insides, which are the only spaces over which some families have any control and keep for themselves, often demonstrate the cultural taste for fine porcelain and cut glass. These insides can be compared with the outside spaces, so often controlled or forced on to Travellers by the 'other' world, from which the Travellers will distance themselves by being unwilling to take responsibility for them. In this context it is interesting to visit privately owned family sites and see there a similar pride in the upkeep of both inside and outside. (For an in-depth study of the 'inside' and the 'outside' see Okely 1983.)

There is now beginning to be a new pride and a willingness among Gypsy Travellers to be identified for what they are. We can see it in Charles Smith's collections of poems (Smith 1995), in the work of the several Gypsy Traveller led organisations, in a recently published anthology of Gypsy writers (Hancock *et al.* 1998) and in the Declaration of Bibi Anisha:

> It is necessary to promote and provide information for and about Roma…. Provide for the teaching of Romani language and history by Roma scholars themselves…. For their part Roma should undertake to communicate information between themselves and with the public authorities through the press, radio, television, conferences, festivals… with the aim of correcting mistaken stereotypes and to eliminate the stigma of being MARGINAL. (Anisha 1997, p.20–21)

A similar mood can be traced right across Europe among Gypsy Travellers who have had some formal education. The growth of Gypsy Traveller/Roma organisations fighting for rights and recognition is fully charted by Jean-Pierre Liégeois . He points out the paradox of Gypsies having to adopt non-Gypsy procedures and ways of organising themselves in order to assert their rights not to be assimilated with non-Gypsies: 'In order to remain Gypsy, it is essential to organise and the only way to do so with any chance of success against the non-Gypsy is to learn to use the same tools he employs' (Liégeois 1994, p.262).

This inevitably creates a tension within Gypsy Traveller groups, between those who feel that this is the only way forward in the modern world and those who prefer to rely on old ways of avoiding confrontations, keeping a low profile and surviving on an individual family basis.

So it is clear that the improving access to schooling, the increasing numbers of children of the current generation who are becoming literate, the greater sense of interculturalism in education are all hugely significant at this time. Factors are converging to offer today's Gypsy Traveller schoolchildren an unprecedented opportunity not only to assert their own identities but also to give their culture a voice and a direction, to enable it to adapt positively to the society with which it now deals.

For several years teachers employed within Traveller Education Services across the country have been working with Gypsy and other Traveller families to get new culturally based resource materials into schools which would provide accurate representations of the various travelling groups. (There has already been some discussion of this in an earlier chapter of this book.) By 1991 John Singh was able to say in a keynote speech to a European conference:

> there now seems to me to be an increasing recognition that all teachers need to be trained to take into account the plurality of the societies in

which they teach whatever the diversity in individual classrooms. As this increasingly happens it should be possible to witness an increase in the contribution that Travellers and other minorities are able to make to the intellectual, aesthetic and cultural developments in individual countries and internationally. (Singh 1991, p.105)

Already in the mid 1970s the then National Gypsy Education Council (now the Gypsy Council for Education, Culture, Welfare and Civil Rights), an organisation with both Traveller and non-Traveller members, had coordinated the publication of a series of anthologies of poems and stories by Traveller children. Since then there have been several others produced by Traveller Education Services with children's work coming from many areas. Resources of all kinds have been produced, seeking not only to allow Gypsy and other Traveller children to find their own cultures represented when they go into classrooms, but also to offer the chance for greater understanding by all children. At the moment the majority of these resources are produced on a small scale with limited print runs and circulation. There still needs to be a realisation by the major educational publishers that such materials are produced for use by *all* children to add to their understanding of minority groups within a multicultural society. Some materials are being produced, but in most cases it is non-Travellers who continue to produce them. It is only gradually – it seems far too slowly – that the steps are being taken away from dependence on the teachers and others to produce the cultural resources, towards young Travellers being able to produce their own statements and products.

If I give a description of that gradual movement in the area where I work, I have no doubt that it will be similar to what has been going on in many other parts of the country. From the early days of our Traveller Education Service we would talk with parents and ask permission, for example, to take photographs of homes, of trailers, of family events, to use bits of family history for translation into educational resources to use with their own and other children. We were never refused, but were very aware of a consciousness of past exploitation, particularly where photographs were concerned. I was told on more than one occasion of people who had come to take photographs, promised to return with prints, but had never been seen again. The families never knew what use had been made of the pictures or what money had been made out of them. We took great care always to explain what we would like the pictures for, what we would do with them and made sure that families not only had prints of any photographs taken, but saw the final products when they were ready for use in schools. Although we acted with integrity, nevertheless we were still only doing what had always been done – we were presenting someone else's culture.

It became clear that many of the children and parents were quite capable of being much more fully involved in the making of the resources and in fact were interested to be so. With the adults we gradually found a greater willingness to take part. This I believe was partly to do with our own increasing familiarity to the families – an understanding of what the purpose of the work was and what the resulting resources would be used for. Also it was, I am sure, a reflection of the changing times – the will now to put their point of view to a wider world in their own way. We could begin to see the developing parent/teacher relationships having direct benefit for the children. With some of the adults it was necessary for the teacher to act as scribe, but more and more of the children were able to do a large part of the work for themselves. Given an opportunity to present aspects of their own culture they found it motivating and stimulating work. I have described three projects in detail elsewhere (Kiddle 1996) in which teenage Travellers took a central role in producing cultural resources. In the first a group of Gypsy Traveller teenagers took photographs of themselves, learned to process and print them and held an exhibition in an arts centre of the images they chose to present to the outside world. For this project I provided the coordination and an art student provided technical assistance. In the second project teenage boys from the fairground community made detailed technical drawings with written explanations and photographs of the design and building up of their family rides, the Waltzer, the Big Wheel and the Noah's Ark. They told of their families' history and tradition in the fairground business. A teacher from the TES oversaw the work and provided assistance with the computer technology in the presentation phase. The third project centred on the work of a teenage Gypsy Traveller, who through drawings and text, on which he collaborated with his father, told the story of the changing life of his family through four generations. The teacher input was in the initiation of the project, the basic structuring of the text and enabling the print run. In all these projects the enhancement of the young people's self-esteem as they were able to take control of the images of themselves that were presented was plain to see.

It was still teachers who were provoking the projects, however, and it was hard to see how there could be a move forwards from this without the teachers continuing to be the initiators. One afternoon in 1996 when I was visiting a site, a van I did not recognise was parked there. As I was leaving two young Traveller women whom I had never seen before called to me from the van and asked if I was the teacher who had helped some Travellers to write their family history? Among the extensive kinship networks, communications are both swift and far reaching. They asked if I could help them. The next day I called at the bungalow where the sisters lived with their mother and looked at the research they had already done. Through talking with the older family members, visiting record offices and checking registers of births and deaths they had already traced relations back to the beginning of the nineteenth century. I asked what they needed me for. They explained that they had thought it would make their family tree more interesting if they got some of the older surviving relatives to tell a few stories from their early lives into a tape recorder; they had already begun with one or two. Did I think this would be a good idea?

It was obvious that all they needed from me was encouragement to have confidence in themselves and what they were doing. I was fascinated to know what had got them started. The younger woman told me that she had never liked school much, but as her mother had settled down after she was widowed, she had had no choice but to go to primary school and she had learned to read and write. Secondary school she seemed to have avoided and as she grew up she started to work with one of her older sisters. She had always been interested in her family heritage and the days when they were all travelling, even though others in the extended family who had also settled down preferred to forget those days entirely. It had started as a hobby, but as she found out more and more her interest grew and now she was thinking of eventually publishing her findings.

I found a family tree of a Gypsy Traveller family which had been prepared by a local head teacher from school records of children who had been in and out of her school in the same locality over five generations. At one extreme edge of this family tree we found cousins to the sisters engaged in their research. Also I was able to show them journals from the 'Romany and Traveller Family History Society', which had been founded in 1994 to provide:

> a network of people like ourselves – that is to say people who have
> both an interest in their family's history and who also have Romany or
> Traveller ancestry... we share something else too: a pride in knowing
> that some of our forbears were 'Gypsies' of one kind or another....
> (Doyle 1994, p.3)

That is surely another sign of the times, when sedentary people begin to take a pride in a Gypsy ancestry.

In the summer of 1997 I went on holiday to County Cork in the South of Ireland and decided to try to find an Irish Traveller family whom I had last seen in England ten years before. For four years during the 1980s the family had periodically travelled through the South West region and I had come to know the family well, particularly the four youngest children who were then of school age. Tracey, the youngest of all, was seven when I first knew her. The first year the family was able to stop in one place for two months and there was chance for reasonable school attendance. As soon as Tracey went in to her classroom her eyes lit up as she looked around at what must have seemed to her a treasure house of books and toys, apparatus and paints. When the family moved on her class teacher remarked, 'That girl could go on to university, you know her enthusiasm for learning is extraordinary'. Each year the family returned, for a few days, weeks or months; they had no permanent base and were travelling throughout England. By the time she was eleven Tracey was fluent in both reading and writing and then the family returned to Ireland, to stay in her grandparents' yard in Cork, I heard.

Ten years later, following up a chain of relations and phone numbers, I found some of the family at the yard in Cork and a few days later met Tracey again at

Puck Fair in Kilorglin. She had been married for two years, but had no children yet. 'I'm not going to have any children for a while' she announced to me soon after we met, 'I want to write a book about my family first'. By talking to her grandparents she already has stories from the lives of her great great grandparents travelling in Wales originally and later in Ireland, and she has begun to write them down.

Later in the summer at a conference on secondary education I found that two teenage Gypsy Traveller girls were running workshops by themselves. These few stories are from my own experience. I am sure they could be parallelled in many places. The literate generation is beginning to make itself heard. Of course I could tell other stories of children who were denied their rights, who never got the opportunity to learn in school or to read, who were and are still constantly moved on and ever more frustrated. There are always individuals who stand out, but I believe that the current generation of Traveller children is receiving school education in sufficient numbers for them really to make a difference to how their people are seen. They will understand that reading and writing are not just for road signs and filling in forms. However, they can only do it if teachers enable them to gain the literacy skills and have high expectations for them, parents give them the opportunities and the support, and both give them the confidence in themselves to use the skills and the opportunities. If the children are given the chance to get all they can from school education they will be able to give voice to the cultural education that they have been given by their families. Instead of parents fearing that schooling will take their sense of their culture away, they should have the courage to help children get the skills from school they need to give a stronger voice to their culture.

The alternatives are acutely depressing. J.-P. Liégeois spells out a bleak scenario:

> if the challenges of everyday living demand every ounce of one's strength and ingenuity (to find a place to stop, to get accommodation, to work, to cope with constant rejection), little is left over for social and cultural development.... Broader interests (artistic expression, education, even political organisation) become luxuries when each day is a battle to remain oneself and to protect what little is left. This is when tradition becomes ritual, having lost its dynamism along the way; it is transformed from a supporting role for identity and lifestyle into a rigid identity in itself, a sort of last refuge. Because of this, the most 'traditional' individuals and groups are not always the most 'authentic', as the stereotype would have us believe: they may be those whose development and adaptability have been blocked, and who, unable to go forward, are treading water as the only alternative to drowning. (Liégeois 1994, p.113)

And Bibi Anisha urges the Gypsy Traveller people to take up the challenge of being responsible for their own destiny:

> If Roma are not able to give a new impetus to the recovering of their cultural identity, it may be that half of them disappear in the anonymity of the surrounding populations and the rest become attracted by criminal and anti-social behaviour. (Anisha 1997, p.21)

The argument being made in this book for Traveller children to be given the power, through the mutual support of their parents and teachers, to better be able to control their own futures is made with an acute awareness of the tensions of the present. The violence now being directed at the Roma in Eastern Europe is driving many to desperate action. If a wider European context is considered, which the next chapter will aim to do, it only seems more urgent.

CHAPTER NINE

A European Perspective

As I was writing the first draft of this chapter in late 1997 the English newspapers were full of stories of hundreds of Gypsies from the Czech Republic and Slovakia arriving in Dover as asylum seekers. Almost a year later they are still coming, by ship and plane. If we consider the statistics published in facts sheets by the Refugee Council it appears likely that they will be denied refugee status, as other Gypsies (notably from Poland) have been denied before them, and they will be returned to eastern Europe (Refugee Council 1996). Their claims of racial persecution will probably not be accepted. The Foreign Secretary was quoted in the *Guardian* as saying:

> We will dutifully and honourably carry out our international obligations to genuine asylum seekers, but I do give a very clear message that Britain does not have an open-door policy to those who may allege persecution and cannot then prove it. (*Guardian*, 28 November 1997)

This reaction seeming to deny the likelihood of racial persecution being proved comes as a response to an increasing awareness among politicians throughout a Europe, preparing to open its doors to the east, that the huge changes which have taken place since 1989 in eastern Europe have had repercussions on the Roma (the name by which central and eastern European Gypsy peoples prefer to be called) which were not anticipated and for which few are prepared. The European Commission (EC) puts a minimum estimate of the number of Gypsies and Travellers in the European Union at 1,500,000. If they look at Europe as a whole their minimum estimate is 7,000,000 (Commission of the European Communities 1996). The issue of the treatment of the Roma has to be faced. Margaret Brearley points to the full seriousness of the situation in a policy paper for the Institute for Jewish Policy Research:

> In September 1994 the CSCE and CE jointly held a major Human Dimension Seminar on Roma in Warsaw. It strongly recommended appointing a mediator to prevent violence against Roma, arguing that anti-Gypsy violence ultimately threatens relations between states (because of its potential for triggering mass migration). (Brearley 1996, p.37)

It is not realistic or helpful for me to write about the Traveller/non-Traveller educational dynamic in England and how this affects the children without setting it in a wider European context. Roma/Gypsy children from Poland, from Slovakia, from the Czech Republic and from Bosnia are in the UK today. Increasingly English and Irish Gypsies and Travellers are travelling on the continent to attend religious conventions, to find work, to take aid to Roma in Romania and to avoid harassment in this country. Showmen are taking fairs to all parts of the world. In attempting to offer a brief contemporary European perspective here I am acutely aware that I rely heavily on the direct experience and scholarship of others (Brearley 1996; Fonseca 1995; Fraser 1992; Liégeois 1994; Liégeois and Gheorghe 1995; Project on Ethnic Relations 1992–1997). I hope that the simple overview that follows will serve to interest others to look at the issues more deeply in other books, reports and papers such as those listed above and learn more as I have done.

In the mid 1980s governments in western Europe had no doubts that the Gypsy Traveller groups had been persecuted and were beginning to accept that the centuries of violence, repression and marginalisation had left those groups in an intolerable position. Education had to be the key issue on which to move. The European Commission asked the Gypsy Research Centre of the Université René Descartes in France to undertake a study on the state of school provision for Gypsy and Traveller children in the participating countries. The study, coordinated by Jean-Pierre Liégeois, took place between 1985 and 1988 and was parallelled by a study undertaken by Ludo Knaepkens into school provision for fairground, circus and bargee children, who were jointly named Occupational Travellers for the purpose of the research.

The study of education provision for Gypsy and Traveller children discovered that over 700,000 such children in the community were getting little or no schooling and that half the members of the Gypsy and Traveller families were under the age of sixteen (Commission of the European Communities 1996, paras. 7 and 10). It was also maintained that school education was becoming a necessary survival tool for Gypsy groups as it had never been before:

> Gypsies' and Travellers' age-old adaptability is currently being tried to the limits, and established strategies for actively adapting to their environment are becoming inadequate.... In the world today the least activity, particularly of an economic nature, demands a minimum grasp of reading, writing and arithmetic. Illiteracy no longer provides protection from the aggression of other cultures as channelled through the school and what is taught there, but becomes a serious handicap in an environment in which the written word is an omnipresent, unavoidable reality.

> Lack of schooling is a serious handicap for economic reasons, but equally serious for social and psychological reasons as well; for

example, dependence on the social services, a situation which is incompatible with the Gypsy's legitimate pride in handling his own, and his [sic] children's affairs....

In other words, the future of Gypsy and Traveller communities depends to a large degree on the schooling available to their children. Active adaptation to the environment, in social as well as economic terms, today requires a grasp of certain basic elements which enable one to analyse and comprehend a changing reality. On the cultural plane these same elements can serve as tools for those wishing to preserve, affirm and develop their own unique identity. (Commission of the European Communities 1996, paras. 11 and 12)

It was quite clear that across the whole of Western Europe as in the UK, the level of prejudice and scant access to school was such that open door approaches were totally insufficient and a proactive response to the findings of the studies was necessary. There were follow up conferences on teacher training and discussions on both the studies to determine the best ways forward.

In 1988 a European platform to represent the educational interests of the Occupational Travellers was formed – the European Federation for the Education of the Children of the Occupational Travellers (EFECOT) – to be directed from Brussels by Ludo Knaepkens who had carried out the original study (this has already been referred to in Chapter 6). This was followed in May 1989 by Resolutions adopted by the countries within the European Commission to promote education and school provision for children of Gypsies, Travellers and Occupational Travellers (Commission of the European Communities 1989). The Resolutions were to have a significant effect, not only by recognising at the level of the EC the need for action and by encouraging member states to take positive measures within their own countries, but also by providing a European budget for projects within intercultural education.

Projects to promote educational opportunities for Occupational Travellers were in the majority of cases channelled and coordinated through EFECOT. My own county's video project, to promote communication between teachers and parents within the fairground community, as described in an earlier chapter, was one of the early actions supported by this budget. Over four or five years EFECOT managed projects in a wide range of areas, from pre-school initiatives for bargee toddlers, to vocational training for young Showmen; from giving information and support to parents, to looking at the conditions in the boarding houses used by some Occupational Traveller families to enable continuous education for their children whilst the parents were travelling. Research was supported to devise a parent held pan-European follow-up record-keeping system and to use the latest technologies in delivering distance learning. The development of EFECOT and the increasing number of partners involved in the several projects from right across western Europe is charted in the yearly work plans submitted to the Commission, a magazine *Newsline*, annual conferences and a congress every third year to evaluate progress.

The actions taken and projects supported from the portion of the budget earmarked for the promotion of educational provision for Gypsies and Travellers are documented in *Interface* magazine which is published by the Centre de Recherches Tsiganes at the Université René Descartes. Through a reading of the quarterly issues of *Interface* a picture can be built up of the various educational activities that have been undertaken across the European Community since the Resolutions of 1989. Profiles of individual countries in turn have allowed each one to describe problems and initiatives, plans and actions mostly from an extremely low baseline and very recent starting points. It is as if a consciousness of the extent of the exclusion of Gypsy Traveller children from school education is only just beginning to be allowed to emerge at the political level.

Many practitioners, teachers, project workers, action researchers and others applied to the delegated part of the intercultural budget to carry out small-scale projects to advance their work with Gypsy and Traveller children. Reading brief reports of the projects across Europe (outreach work, developing culturally relevant teaching materials, promoting distance learning, teaching Gypsy and Traveller cultures to children in schools, study visits, exchanges) and hearing of work in progress from colleagues in this country, I have the impression of some intensely hard work in extremely difficult working conditions on meagre budgets. Sometimes one project seems to duplicate another and it was difficult in the beginning to find a framework for coordination or quality evaluation at a level below the overall supervision by a group known as the Ad Hoc Group made up of one or two delegates from each member state.

To offer a central resource, a database of contacts, research and materials is being built up at the *Interface* office to provide the access point for a future network of those working in the same field. This database should be invaluable for all those who are able to have access to it. However, it presupposes not only literacy but also IT competence and availability for those who wish to use it themselves directly as opposed to as mediated by office staff. It provides another demonstration of the fact that if Roma, Gypsy and Traveller groups wish to take an active part in the debate about the education of their children, they will have to be versed in the ways and skills of the educators in order to do so.

The team at the Centre de Recherches Tsiganes has also initiated a series of publication projects. The Interface Collection is a series of new books dealing with aspects of Gypsy history in Europe, Romani linguistics and reference works, for school and scholarly use. One of the most recent is an encyclopaedia project (described fully in *Interface*, no. 23, August 1996) which is being developed to offer information, items and articles from a Roma/Gypsy perspective in several languages including a Standardised Romani. The encyclopaedia project is an exciting one in that it seeks co-operation and input from members of the communities themselves (inevitably the literate ones) in its development:

> this Encyclopaedia will be, not an Encyclopaedia about Gypsies and Travellers, but rather an Encyclopaedia for Gypsies and Travellers, which includes topics of general interest analysed and presented from a Gypsy point of view, as well as items of more particular relevance to the Gypsy/Traveller historical, cultural, linguistic etc. world.... It will fulfil a pedagogical/informational function, but also one of sens- itisation, not only for Gypsies and Travellers themselves but also for other interested readers. It must be a tool for inter-community communication, understanding and respect. (Liégeois 1996, p.11)

Through *Interface* magazine and conference reports from the Project on Ethnic Relations, it is possible to catch the edges of an intense debate that has been going on between Roma scholars and scholars of Romani about committing Romani to a standardised form for writing. Probably the most significant contributions to this debate have come from eastern European Roma scholars. Under Communism Gypsy ethnicity was denied as part of policies of forced settlement, assimilation and education. Families were settled in groups on the margins of communities and employed mainly in agricultural collectives and factories in manual jobs. Looking back to those times participants in the current Project on Ethnic Relations (PER) observe that though the assimilation policies were thoroughly pursued, for the majority there was rarely a positive outcome: 'While policies of forced assimilation did not achieve their stated goals, they were successful in a purely negative sense: they destroyed traditional social structures, occupational skills and values without providing replacements' (PER Report 1992, p.14).

A small minority, however, were able to take advantage of educational opportunities and as a result there is in eastern Europe an educated elite of well qualified and articulate Roma teachers, lawyers and other professional people who are willing to identify themselves and are able to make a huge contribution to the increasingly political movement to affirm Roma ethnic identity and rights.

> In traditional Romani communities, intellectuals were non existent: without a written language and culture, education was not a basic value. Moreover, many Romani families, fearing assimilation, were reluctant to press their children to become educated. For others, lack of resources was a major obstacle to obtaining an education. The thin stratum of Romani intellectuals presently active in Europe is thus of recent origin, the result of coercive educational measures undertaken since the 1950s, mostly in the former communist states. (Mirga and Gheorghe 1997, p.13)

For these educated Roma the issue of language is central. Even though the majority of Roma are not literate and the existence of many different dialect forms of Romani make the task of agreeing on a standardised version to be used in writing fraught with difficulty and dissension, nevertheless it is with a common language that the Roma scholars believe they and others of their community can reaffirm the Roma ethnic identity. The argument of Nicolae Gheorghe, a Romanian Roma, is recorded in a PER conference report:

> the Roma, as Gheorghe explained, are undergoing a process of ethnogenesis – from a despised marginal community known as tsiganis to a recognised ethnic minority known as the Roma. In view of this fact, it is not surprising that much of the discussion was centred upon language issues and the need to standardise the Romani language. There was general agreement that, as a defining characteristic of ethnicity, a single unified language was an important tool for strengthening ethnic identity and for facilitating communication among members of the ethnic group. (PER Report 1992, p.14)

A group of Gypsy intellectuals from across Europe had founded the International Romani Union several years previously to seek to bring an awareness of the fate of half a million Gypsies in the Holocaust and the continuing struggles and marginalisation of their peoples to wider public attention. The first meeting of what was called the World Gypsy Congress was held in London in 1971. However, it is the events which have followed the break up of communism triggered by the revolutions in 1989 which have given a new urgency to the debate.

In 1989, when the EC passed the Resolutions to promote educational opportunities for Occupational Travellers and Gypsy Travellers in western Europe, there can have been little understanding of what the overturning of the communist regimes would mean for the Roma peoples in the east. As the countries of eastern Europe began to reshape themselves and come to terms with the economic stresses and wide unemployment which arrived with the new market approaches, the Roma became victims in more than one way following the rise of nationalism. As factories closed, the Roma, forced into them under assimilation policies, were among the first to be unemployed, but now they had few of their traditional trades or skills to fall back on and were in many cases reduced to destitution:

> If forced settlement and the denial of traditional trades during the communist period led the majority of Roma into positions of unskilled labour in factories and agricultural co-operatives, then the economic restructuring of the 1990s has resulted in unemployment for a large portion of the Roma. (Tanaka 1997 p.3)

Living in often desperate conditions and struggling to survive, sometimes even having to abandon children, the Roma found themselves victimised again as the lowest of social groupings and used by others to give vent to their own angers and anxieties in the newly emerging states. Intensified hostility and violence has characterised the attitude of non-Roma towards the Roma, violence which has led to several murders and widespread fear. Nicolae Gheorghe spoke to the British press: 'Before the revolution, only the police were violent to Romanies. Now the whole population can be' (*The Times*, 30 September 1992). Livia Plaks, writing the preface to a PER conference report, sums up the situation:

> After the fall of Communism in Central and Eastern Europe, violence against the Roma erupted with a vehemence that took many governments and the Roma by surprise. Faced with the multiple stresses and insecurities of economies and societies in transition, many in the majority populations found the politically and economically marginalised Roma an all too inviting target for scapegoating. (Plaks 1997, p.1)

For the Roma it is a time of crisis. Some live in appalling poverty in fear of the attacks of skinhead gangs. Others have begun migrations westwards, trying to escape persecution and find a way to improve their standard of living. Groups of Roma travelling into Germany and other western European countries have found little respite. Coming as they do to countries still only at the beginnings of recognising the needs of the Gypsy Traveller groups who have already been in western Europe for generations, the presence of the eastern European Roma only complicates the issues that are starting to be acknowledged. Speaking only Romani and/or languages of the eastern European countries from which they have come, the need for translation is another complicating factor, particularly when translators may themselves have little sympathy or concern for the situation of the Roma. Under arrangements made between European countries many of the Roma have already been returned to the countries from which they came most recently.

Some families, forcibly settled, their culture suppressed and their ethnicity denied during the Communist era, have decided to make a virtue of assimilation and no longer identify themselves as ethnic Roma. The situation of Slovakia may be used as an example. A study commissioned by the Minority Rights Group (Liégeois and Gheorghe 1995) estimated that there are approximately 500,000 Roma in Slovakia today. However, city councils throughout Slovakia reported in another study that in 1989 approximately 254,000 Roma were then living in the country. In the 1991 Slovak census in which citizens identify themselves, the figure for Roma was 75,802 (Cahn and Trehan 1997). Many, many families are clearly unwilling to identify themselves officially as Roma fearing the hostility, stigmatisation and possible violence which would follow. The European Roma Rights Center [sic] (ERRC), which has been set up to monitor the human rights situation of the Roma points out how this contributes in many instances to a denial by the authorities that there is a racist dimension to known acts of violence. The ERRC considers 'the failure to recognise the racial character of crimes against Roma in legal terms to be one of the important aspects of the denial of Roma rights in Slovakia' (Cahn and Trehan 1997, p.35).

The same point is made in the Project on Ethnic Relations' reports: 'There has been a marked reluctance on the part of national and local authorities to recognise the ethnic nature of anti-Romani violence, and they have tended to underplay the frequently racist character of some incidents' (Plaks 1997, p.1).

The Roma intellectuals have to face this complex issue head on. Their work to bring the condition, needs and rights of the ethnic minority group, the Roma, to public attention for them to be recognised and addressed is made the more difficult when so many have been and are denying themselves. The issue of representation is complicated for the intellectuals who find both uneducated Roma and state officials questioning their 'authenticity'. Some of those who hid themselves before, but now come out and claim their heritage and identity face challenges from all sides. Nicolae Gheorghe examines this in his own writings:

> There exists a stratum of Romani people integrated into society who are able to maintain a dialogue with the different establishments – political, administrative and academic – who nonetheless suspect that we are not 'true Gypsies' because we no longer live in the traditional conditions which are documented by ethnographers and anthropologists.
>
> There is therefore a crisis of legitimacy for our (i.e. Romani intellectuals') own 'ethnic identity', towards our own constituency which sometimes refuses credit and in the questions of the 'Gaje' establishment regarding who exactly we are. (Gheorghe 1997, p.157)

As Roma intellectuals from eastern Europe and also from America have begun to create a higher profile for their people in the political arena it has become ever clearer that formal educational opportunities are of central importance to Roma/Gypsy peoples. If these opportunities when taken are coupled with a willingness to assert an ethnic identity, to take hold of the 'Gypsy image' and work to remove it from the stereotypes that non-Gypsies have created, others will have confidence in time to do the same.

Back in England in 1991 Peter Mercer, an English Gypsy Traveller, gave a presentation to a European education conference acknowledging the potential power of determined, articulate Roma/Gypsies working together across Europe:

> Without adequate education we as Gypsy people are going to find it difficult to co-ordinate with other Gypsy groups across Europe. In the new Europe of federal states it may mean that there needs to be a concerted effort by Gypsy people as a whole to combat injustice and to demand fair treatment. Education should create a demand and interest

to learn amongst Gypsy people about the history, language and culture of our people. We should study our past and our language. We want more of our people educated so that we can have more of our people representing us in the Parliaments and Councils in Europe. It was pointed out to me that it is a sad fact that it's only through education we can impress on the world our legitimate worth and right of being. (Mercer 1991, p.12)

The European Commission had requested that at the end of 1993 all member states should report back on the progress that they had made in implementing the 1989 resolutions. It would be a time to take stock and plan future actions. The final reports from the Commission, which brought together the information provided by the reports from individual member states, were not published until the end of 1996.

However it was quite clear that the pressing needs identified in the research leading to the resolutions would take many years to tackle and individual projects and initiatives would require time to produce discernible results. The Commission therefore reinforced its commitment to improve the educational opportunities of Gypsies, Travellers and Occupational Travellers in 1995 when launching the SOCRATES programme, with a remit to fund education projects for five years. Some actions within the chapters of SOCRATES are specifically targeted at Gypsy and Traveller groups and this budget has enabled many projects to take place. The European dimension is stressed in the criteria which project proposals must meet, with a demand for at least two or three countries to work in partnership in each project.

Also, 1994 saw the publication in English of Jean-Pierre Liégeois' book, *Roma, Gypsies, Travellers* (Liégeois 1994), which, updating previous publications, gives a full overview of the groups throughout Europe together with detailed documentation of the changing patterns and perspectives. Anyone who still holds a simple stereotype of a 'true Gypsy' would have it dispelled once and for all by a reading of this book which maps out a complex mosaic of interdependent groupings of families, extended family groups, cultures and societies. There is both pessimism and possibility within this book, reflecting the opportunities being created at national and international level which often fail to have the force desired because of the continued prejudice on the ground.

At an international level, step by small step the Roma political activists are gaining recognition – in 1995 the UN recognised the Roma as an official minority – and there is a greater understanding now of the scale of Roma/Gypsy suffering under the Nazi regime in the Second World War. Finally, in 1996, the European Commission published its reports on the measures taken by member states in response to the 1989 resolutions. In setting the context of the report on educational provision for Gypsy and Traveller children the low base line of the starting point discovered by the research carried out in the 1980s was reiterated. There has been some progress and some grounds for optimism:

> In many ways Gypsies and Travellers demonstrate better adaptation to present changes, and to future ones, than other sections of the population: their economic flexibility, geographic mobility, and in-family education, their communal lifestyle linking the individual into a network of reciprocal security and giving him a solid identity. Their society is young, with as many children as adults. Bit by bit families are taking on more books and schooling is on the rise. The children will read – and then they will write, enriching European culture with their contributions. These children must have the opportunity to get into school, to stay in school, and to be personally and culturally respected while there. (Commission of the European Communities 1996, p.8, para.14)

Country by country actions and initiatives are detailed in the report. The Commission points to a number of the programmes which it has developed over years that have a direct relevance to school provision for Gypsy and Traveller children (ibid., p.11–12, para. 22) – programmes:

- to combat illiteracy and scholastic failure;
- to promote equal educational opportunity and reduce disparities;
- to introduce new technologies (which can be relevant to distance learning);
- for teacher training and information exchange.

There are many opportunities for national and local authorities, schools and organisations to bid for funding under these programmes (if they can deal with the paper work!) to continue enlarging and consolidating the provisions they are making for Gypsy and Traveller groups.

The Commission sees education as the 'linchpin' in EU activity and concludes this report with an unequivocal restatement of entitlement: 'The right to schooling applies to all children, unconditionally, and must be put into practice with an eye to ensuring equal opportunity and in a context guaranteeing respect for the child's culture' (ibid., p.88, para. 325).

Immediately afterwards, however, in the following paragraph the report sounds a note of caution:

> Considerable distance has been covered in a single generation. We must, however, bear in mind that, if part of the road is being travelled, and the jigsaw of projects and programmes in diverse and essential domains is gradually taking shape, a great deal nonetheless remains to be done, and that in a difficult context rendering all progress fragile and uncertain. (ibid., p.88, para. 326)

Yes indeed it is a 'difficult context' and there is so much more to be done. If we take this report and Liégeois' book together we can see that across western Europe at an overall policy level attempts are being made to give educational and other opportunities to Gypsy and Traveller peoples. About time, one might say, after some six centuries of harsh and repressive, at times genocidal, treatment. But we can also see, at the local level, the legacy of those six centuries in the extremes of prejudice that remain which often hinder the children from making the most of the opportunities that are there.

In England we cannot be complacent. Whilst the impetus towards access to the opportunities of school education began here in the late 1960s, earlier than in some other countries of Europe, nevertheless the Specific Grant funding for Traveller Education Services, put in place in 1990 as a coherent initiative after the 1989 resolutions, has not kept pace with the assessed and monitored needs of the children. The percentage of funding made available by central government has shrunk from 75 per cent to 65 per cent leaving local authorities with increasingly difficult choices to make about the allocation of resources. Always at local level there is the gut hostility to be overcome.

In Slovakia there is national legislation in place which should protect the rights of the individual. This does not prevent anti-Roma racist violence from taking place on the streets, where police officers seem less than rigorous in preventing it. There does not seem to be political will at a senior level to enforce the national legislation at a local level (Cahn and Trehan 1997). We could make a parallel with the 1968 Caravan Sites Act, brought into force in England to oblige local authorities to make adequate site accommodation available for Gypsy Traveller families. Central government created the duty and the opportunity and later the money for site building, but the level of hostility in each neighbourhood from non-Gypsies was the overwhelming factor, identified in the 1977 Cripps Report, which made site building so slow, and local politicians had little will to push unpopular measures through. Similarly at the level of government there was a reluctance to enforce the legislation by the direction of local authorities to provide sites, which the Act gave them power to do.

If education is the key, it is not just the education of Gypsy and Traveller children that we have to think about. In her policy paper, which examines the situation of the Roma/Gypsies in Europe, Margaret Brearley makes the education of *all* an issue of central importance (Brearley 1996). She reports some of the proposals made in 1995 by the European Parliament's Consultative Commission on Racism and Xenophobia (European Parliament 1995).

These proposals recommend that education authorities should make sure that within all educational institutions from school to university level there is a commitment to deal with anti-Gypsy prejudice as part of the general framework of multicultural and anti-racist education. The proposals suggest that the teaching of Gypsy culture and history become part of an intercultural curriculum and point out how vital the role of the teacher is in countering prejudice among young people. The necessity for initial and in-service training for teachers in this area is highlighted together with the importance of appropriate materials being available as resources for the work. It is recommended that concern for the treatment of Gypsy and Traveller groups be an integral part of all policies to deal with bullying and racial harassment in and around schools.

These recommendations demonstrate also the need for teachers, mediators and resource materials to come from within the Roma, Gypsy and Traveller communities themselves, which returns us to the discussion of the previous chapter in this book.

At the highest levels of European politics the extent of anti-Gypsy feeling is well known and countries are urged to make policies which will come to terms with this and begin to alter attitudes at the local level. The huge scale of this task, which obviously demands persistent long-term commitment by a whole range of agencies together with appropriate resourcing for there to be any chance of success, is daunting. Particularly when a media story, picking up an isolated incident and reinforcing a stereotype, can so easily further entrench public perceptions of Roma and Gypsy people.

Yet there was international surprise expressed (to go back to the story with which I began this chapter) when television documentaries showing Roma/Gypsy Travellers living comfortably in Canada and Britain provoked sudden large migrations by Roma families from the Czech Republic and Slovakia. The response went along the lines of: the eastern European countries had laws to protect citizens, therefore the Roma could not be so persecuted as they claimed, therefore their motives had to be economic. This despite the research, the concern for positive action against prejudice, the proposals for dealing with anti-Gypsy racism that have been briefly documented in this chapter. The migrations of Roma families from the east, at a time when western governments have still not come to terms with the needs of Gypsy Traveller groups who have long been in western Europe, are providing circumstances that governments are not appearing ready to confront.

Grasping that nettle – acknowledging, confronting and beginning to deal with the prejudice at local level – is a daunting prospect for any government. As 1997 was designated the European Year against racism, this could have afforded many opportunities. In Britain the Commission for Racial Equality toured a magnificent exhibition – 'Roots of the Future' – ethnic diversity in the making of Britain. Sadly there was no Gypsy Traveller element in this exhibition. The book (Commission for Racial Equality 1997) serving as a permanent extension of the exhibition mentions Gypsies briefly only in the historical section when the first immigrants arrived in Tudor times. There is nothing of the present day Gypsy Traveller population who are so often hidden from official reports and statistics within a 'white' category. In the way the census forms are presented, 'ethnic minorities' are those who do not identify themselves as 'white', though this may change. Only when we officially 'see' Gypsy Travellers as an ethnic minority will we be able to form a proper judgement of how our society is treating them, and in particular enabling the children to make the most of themselves.

The child's voice has been lacking from this chapter, dealing as it has with a wide European overview and policies and initiatives at a national and international level. However, it has been made clear that education is seen throughout Europe as the key to increased opportunity and how important the role of the teacher must be. This has to be seen alongside the family opportunity, or lack of it, to have access to and engage positively with formal education. In every European country, as has been explored in more detail in England, mixed messages are being given to parents, which will have to be resolved before parents will be able to support their children in school.

It has been estimated that approximately half of the European Gypsy Traveller population is under sixteen, so the young people could represent a considerable force if they had the opportunities or the forum to make themselves heard. This raises the question of identity and peer group. I have not given much space to peer group issues in this book as its prime focus is the parent/teacher relationship, the adult dynamic, as it inevitably affects the opportunities for the child. To look in detail at every factor which contributes to what a Traveller child experiences in school is beyond the scope and possible length of this book. However, in the international context it is interesting to look at a very few initiatives which have sought to involve young Travellers from various groups directly and offer them a peer group in their wider communities.

In reporting the research into the education of Show children in Queensland, Australia (Danaher 1998) which was described in Chapter 6, Danaher states that attempts by teachers to operate 'buddy systems' in the schools which the Show children attended briefly whilst travelling were not usually successful. He suggests that the Show children had a sufficiently strong peer group among themselves and did not need or want to engage in a contrived system which sought to integrate them with others. It seemed that in uncontrived social situations, such as playing sport, new relationships were much more easily formed. In Europe, there have been some actions to build on the possibilities for identification with a wider peer group, for mobile children who can be isolated and unable to sustain regular relationships with their contemporaries in school.

EFECOT in its work with Occupational Travellers has recognised both this need and the importance of involving young Travellers directly in discussions about their education and their futures. At an EFECOT congress in Luxembourg in 1992, where young Occupational Travellers were brought together to discuss matters important to them, their central message was: 'We want to participate in discussions and decision-making procedures concerning our own future' (EFECOT 1994, p.16).

This led to the formation of the EFECOT Junior organisation, aiming to reach and involve children and young people of rivercraft, fairground and circus parents through a magazine (*Junior News*), activities and the creation of opportunities to meet each other. The study skills magazine project, which was the case study described in Chapter 7 of this book, was another initiative of this kind on a more local level. Recently in Spain, those organising the mobile circus schools in that country have suggested the production of their own magazine with two particular aims – to improve the communications between all pupils, parents and teachers who travel with the circus and to let others, outside the circus business, know more of how it works.

Projects funded under the SOCRATES programme have enabled small youth groups of Gypsy Traveller children to travel to other European countries to visit Roma, Gypsy and Traveller communities living there. For those who continually have to cope with being 'the other', 'the outsider' in their daily dealings with the society around them, these exchanges provide opportunities for relationships and solidarity from a position of shared culture and experience.

With a similar motivation the Union Romani, a Spanish organisation, obtained European funding to hold the 1st European Congress of Roma Youth in Barcelona in November 1997. Those running the congress felt that as the Roma/Gypsy and Traveller peoples were so wide-spread across the world, it was important to create an opportunity for the young generation to meet, share their experiences and try to find ways to protect the Roma/Gypsy Traveller culture and eradicate illiteracy. Discussion groups were held in four areas:

- Education and Social Policy
- Human Rights and Civil Liberties
- Youth Participation, Associationism, Women
- Culture.

A few Gypsy Traveller young people from England were able to attend the Congress. A comment made by one teenage girl was that it was a pity that there were more adults attending the Youth Congress than there were young people. In the context of this book it is perhaps appropriate to end this chapter with this remark.

CHAPTER TEN

Reflecting on Practice

The last chapter of a book should seek to bring together some of the ideas and thoughts that have been visited along the way. Looking back I seem to have made rather a meandering journey, however, and I plan to make two more diversions before I head for home.

The first is provoked by my reading a study of the children in England of Punjabi immigrant parents (Dasanjh and Ghuman 1996). The research is into child-rearing practices and looks at the issues which are central to second and third generation immigrants. I found much that was familiar in the descriptions of parents anxious to maintain the core values of the family and the support of the kinship networks. I recognised families who involved their children in all family activities, letting them be with adults, hear adult conversation, participate with respect. I found a parallel with Gypsy Traveller attitudes also in the Punjabi attitude to individuality. It does not have the same high significance as the freedom to seek and reach individual potential does for many Western people. Of greater importance is the fulfilling of a known and accepted role within the family, the kinship network (known to the Punjabis as the 'biraderi') and the wider community. For the children, growing up and going to school in a Western society, there can be problems: 'This chasm between the value systems of the migrants and that of the host society has posed very serious difficulties for the second generation Asians' (Dasanjh and Ghuman 1996, p.18) 'Some young people can become alienated from both cultures as they face racial discrimination and rejection from the host society and disenchantment with their family's rigid insistence on maintaining traditional values (ibid., p.24).

I have seen all this too. The Punjabi parents in the study recognised that the future security for their children lay in success in the job market and so they encouraged school attendance and academic achievement to qualify their children to compete in tough and often racist environments. They encouraged this knowing the other influences that there would be on the children. The study found parents trying to hold things in balance:

> Punjabi families... are encouraging their children to acquire competencies (knowledge of computers, for instance), social skills and interests which will ensure their success in wider British society. At the same time they are doing their best to pass on the family values and

traditions in order to ensure a degree of continuity of the home culture.
(ibid., p.165)

My second diversion is to Sledderlo, a housing estate a few miles outside the industrial town of Genk in eastern Belgium. The estate has few facilities, is away from the town, hidden by a band of pine trees, and is home in the main to immigrant workers and their families. After the Second World War immigrants were encouraged to come and work in the mines and the factories of this industrial area. Turks, Moroccans, Greeks, Yugoslavs, Italians – people of some fifteen nationalities – all came for the jobs and were housed in Sledderlo. The families stayed, children were born and began to grow up, but gradually the mines and the factories closed down. For many it was impossible to find other work and when I first visited Sledderlo in 1985 over 80 per cent of the young adults (sixteen to twenty-five year olds) on the estate were unemployed.

I was there, during my summer holiday time, to work with my husband and his company on a theatre show with teenagers from the estate. Peter had returned to theatre-based work after our time with ACERT in London and had been in contact with youth workers in Sledderlo since 1982 about the possibility of developing theatre work with the young people on the estate. The youth workers there had found another group of second generation immigrants with all the same feelings of alienation and frustration to deal with. Brought up and schooled in Belgium they wanted to join that society, but it largely rejected them. Many of them rarely, if ever, saw their parents' homelands and had few connections there. Parents tried to keep their own traditions going, but with many cultures together and huge unemployment there was little social stability and the young ones were trying to go their own ways. The teenagers had low self-esteem and were searching for an identity.

The youth workers thought that theatre might be a helpful intercultural medium through which they might develop activities on the estate and had asked Peter, who was now very experienced and a specialist in comm-unity-based theatre work, to come over as adviser, director and animateur and help to get a project underway. On my first visit to Sledderlo, with Peter's company, the Theatre of Public Works (TPW), I was to help run workshops in music and circus skills and create a show with the young people. I had not known what to expect and was extremely nervous, knowing the reputation of the estate, worried about language and translation difficulties, anticipating resentful, tough street kids. It certainly was hard work and nerve wracking, but in the teenage boys we worked with (it was mostly boys as many of the girls were Muslim and not allowed to participate), I found so many similarities in attitude and manner to those of the Gypsy Traveller youngsters I worked with, that I felt quite at home! Language was not a problem either as nearly everyone had some English, mainly learned it seemed through watching American films on television.

The association of TPW with Sledderlo was a productive and continuing one over many years. I joined the projects whenever they coincided with my holiday times and watched as over a period of some five years, under the guidance of their youth workers, the young people first learned skills and helped TPW to make shows, then organised shows jointly with TPW and finally created their own shows with TPW personnel on the sidelines as advisers. A photographic project, 'Speaking for Ourselves', was run in parallel with the theatre work very much on the lines of the project in which Gypsy Traveller teenagers had been involved in England (described in an earlier chapter).

In the first year of the theatre projects in Sledderlo the teenagers had joined in with the workshops, but held back from being involved with the show, which in the end was played to them on the streets of the estate. However, when I was next able to go back a couple of years later, it was to join in on a two week residential theatre camp held away from the estate, down in the Ardennes, during which TPW, the youth workers and both male and female young people from Sledderlo devised and rehearsed a show together, which was then performed back on their home estate. The Belgian youthworkers were both excited and nervous because, although they had organised many single sex camping trips previously, this was the first time that parents had allowed the teenagers to go on a mixed camp. It was crucial to the whole development of the theatre work that nothing should go wrong at the camp. It turned out to be a great success and there was to me a remarkable spirit of co-operation within the group.

It was only years after that camp, when I was talking again to one of the young Moroccan women, who had been a teenager on the camp and had remained involved in the theatre work ever since, that I heard more of the background. We were reminiscing about the fact that she had had to be heavily disguised in her role in the first show as her father had not approved of her participation. She then revealed a second level of secrecy. She told me that the group of teenagers going on the camp had got together in Sledderlo beforehand, without the knowledge of parents or youth workers, and had made an agreement among themselves that no one would cause trouble on the camp. They were all excited by the possibilities that they could see in the theatre projects and were determined not to spoil it for themselves.

Reading Máirín Kenny's study (Kenny 1997) earlier this year, which explores the peer group relationships of young Irish Travellers and their interactions as a group with their teachers, I was reminded of Sledderlo and the power of the peer group to make any situation destructive or constructive.

From the early 1990s the young people of Sledderlo have had their own rehearsal studio and making space and their own theatre company – Yahwar – which has been invited to perform as far away as Japan. In the beginning the contents of the shows were entertainments or fable and myth-based tales of good and evil, battles and reconciliation, but as their confidence grew the subject matter took on issues of power and greed. Three years ago they were able at last to look at their own situation and created a powerful show about the experience of immigrant workers, full of fire, danger, drumming and immense skill. In researching and preparing for this show they interviewed their own parents and heard stories and had conversations that they had never had before. Through theatre this group of young people is beginning to find an identity and voice.

Ayhan, one of the Turkish youths who was with the group from the first project, speaks for himself and many of the others:

> Nu kunnen ze zien dat vreemdelingen ook iets kunnen!
> Ze zien een vreemdeling achter een masker.
>
> Ik voel me Belg,
> doordat ik hier geboren ben, maar
> ik ben een Turk
> en ik voel me ook Turk omdat ik de
> Turkse nationaliteit heb. (Yahwar 1992)

Translation:

> Now they can see that the foreigners can also do something
> They see the foreigner behind the mask.
>
> I feel a Belgian
> because I was born here, but
> I am a Turk
> and I feel a Turk because
> I have Turkish nationality.

I have made these two digressions because there are so many resonances with the circumstances and attitudes of Gypsy Traveller children in the situations of the young people I have described. The significant difference is that the Punjabis studied in England and the young people of Sledderlo are second or at most third generation immigrants whilst Gypsies have been in Britain for 500 years. Yet many of the young Gypsy Travellers I come across seem to be at a similar stage in their relationships to their parents and the wider society. There is a consciousness too, and sometimes a resentment on the part of Gypsy Traveller families that more recent immigrants' needs appear to have been addressed and attended to more swiftly than their own.

For the other immigrant groups I have mentioned, there was the first pressing need to find jobs in the new country. Therefore schooling, language acquisition, achieving qualifications were immediately perceived as necessary. When, as in Sledderlo, the job opportunities fell away, some of the young people intensified their determination to get good qualifications and be fully part of their new country at the expense of their traditions, others began to resent school in its turn, a second level of alienation. For some the theatre group offered another possibility – a move forward on their own terms.

For the Gypsy Travellers in England self-employment, by providing skills, items or services to others in ways which have been passed on through family education, has always been the tradition and the ideal. They have made a virtue of the culture of separateness, of resourcefulness, of mobility, of keeping a low profile in times of repression and intolerance. The base of the culture – the oral tradition and network of kinship support – has been strong. Schooling and literacy have not been necessary in the same way – until now.

For our part, we – the sedentary society – have never quite coped with having a nomadic element to our society. We have used it as a convenient scapegoat when necessary, our literary imaginations and our escapist fantasies have fed on it, we have tried to destroy it or assimilate it when it seemed too threatening, but we have never accepted or accommodated it as a natural element within our society. We have never accepted mobility as, say, the Australians had to accept space and distance and developed distance learning as a matter of course within their education system.

The nature of the working relationship between the Gypsy and the non-Gypsy has meant that however much Gypsy Travellers might have wanted to maintain traditional ways for themselves, as conditions have changed for all of us, we have all had to move on.

Two world wars, the motor car, the coming of television and the other incredible advances in technology in the last hundred years have meant that in the twentieth century each generation of children has had a new world to deal with. No young generation in this century has faced the same conditions as their parents faced. Now literacy and other skills that schools can offer are necessary for Gypsy Traveller children alongside the skills they learn from their families, and all across Europe it is being recognised. Of course schooling will change things for the children and it will change them. Its influence will be one more together with that of parents, of their peer group, of television, of advertising, of the wider society with which the children will have to relate to make their livings. But there is no inevitability about the way the influence of school will be felt. The actions and attitudes of individual schools and individual teachers can have a real significance; therefore it is really important what each one does.

There can be no simple set of guidelines, because for all the differences between teachers and schools, there are comparable differences in attitudes between Gypsy Traveller families themselves. For every family that refuses to let their children near secondary schools fearful of the erosion of their traditional culture, there are others who are quite happy to see the children go and are only disappointed if the experience does not do as much for them as they had hoped. Recently I was telephoned about a woman, now living in a house, who was most anxious not to be identified as a Gypsy. She was convinced that if her son was so identified in the records going with her application for a secondary school place for him, some subtle discrimination would keep him out from the school of her choice. Others are angry if their children are not acknowledged and welcomed for what they are. There is no point in dealing in stereotypes and making generalised assumptions. There can be no substitute for time, sensitivity, talking and individual concern.

At primary level, there can be no doubt there has been an overall shift towards the acceptance of and the opportunity for schooling over the last twenty years. I am now at the stage where young mothers, whom I taught when they were children themselves, are telling me of their own children's experiences in school. The differences in opportunity and attitude are plain to see and I am sure their stories are comparable to those of many others. There is Margaret, the eldest of five children, who started out calling with her mother when she was five years old. When I first met her she was twelve. There had been a period when there were too many young children to be taken out together and Margaret had had two three-month periods in school when the family had stayed in one place for long enough for her parents to consider school worthwhile. She told me that she hadn't had time to learn much because she was usually protecting her little brother (the third in the family) from being bullied in the playground and worrying about him in class on his own. Her other brother (the second in the family) had done the learning, she said. He could read and he taught her in the evenings at home. School had not lasted for long for her because by the age of nine she was considered old enough to stay at home and mind the little ones. That was still her job when I met her and I was not able to get a school place for her as her father would not allow it. Now Margaret is a mother with four children of her own. She has a plot on a site in the north and does not leave it often because if she goes away for more than four weeks at a time the pitch is forfeit and she doesn't like to be away during school terms. The last time I saw her she told me how delighted she was with her seven year old daughter's prowess on the computer and how well her handwriting was coming on. She is determined that her daughter will be able to cope with the world she will have to face.

Kelly, whose parents protected her so much as a young girl and took so much persuasion to let her go to school, tells me that she has her daughter's name down for playgroup and she has arranged for the place to be kept for her if she is away.

Sheena, whose parents were persuaded to let her attend a special school, sends her two children to school without fail every time she is in my area, even if it is only for three or four days.

At secondary level it is not the same, and an earlier chapter has looked at many of the factors coming into play at this stage. The Gypsy/non-Gypsy dynamic is complex and for the children trying to make a coherence for themselves there is not just the generation or two of turmoil faced by other recent immigrant groups in adapting to our schools and our society. Gypsy

Traveller children have to cope with the centuries of history, of which they may be unaware, but which colours every one of our attitudes to them in some way. I have said that it is important what teachers do. I have discussed rights and responsibilities inside and outside school, partnerships and joint participation, mutual support between parents and teachers, but I am not sure how realistic this can be, how idealistic a statement it is. Without a sense of being on equal terms there can be no proper partnership and the possibility of equal terms is denied by present power relationships and the inadequacy of legal accommodation. So the adults engage with each other in a variety of ways, the children's education lies in the middle, and the children themselves are not at all sure where they stand.

We need to look for a terrain on which an idea of equality of concern for the child can take root and be fed by co-operation. Education and pride in themselves is the power that parents and teachers can jointly give to the children – a power to develop self-esteem, a power for choice, a power to defend against exploitation. What it will take from Traveller parents is a courage to identify themselves, to trust schools and to trust their children to take the culture forward. What it will take from teachers is a refusal to tolerate any level or form of prejudice or action which would betray that courage and trust. I have no illusions about the immense difficulties that presents for both parents and teachers, Traveller and non-Traveller, but I do not care to contemplate the alternative future for the children.

I would make the same argument for all children – the necessity for parents and teachers to work together to let the children have the chance to learn from both and then move on to be truly themselves. I would argue for all children that we should listen to what they have to say, because they have to deal with a different world from the one their parents and teachers grew into. I argue it particularly for Gypsy and Traveller children because for them the tensions are greater, the hostility they can face is more intense, the stereotyping is more negative, history weighs more heavily on them and they have been too long at the margins.

Glossary of Acronyms

ACERT	–	Advisory Council for the Education of Romanies and other Travellers
ALBSU	–	Adult Literacy and Basic Skills Unit
CE	–	Council of Europe
CJA	–	Criminal Justice and Public Order Act
DES	–	Department of Education and Science
DFE	–	Department for Education
DfEE	–	Department for Education and Employment
DOE	–	Department of the Environment
EC	–	European Commission
EFECOT	–	European Federation for the Education of the Children of the Occupational Travellers
EO	–	Education Otherwise
ERRC	–	European Roma Rights Center
EU	–	European Union
EWO	–	Education Welfare Officer
GCECWCR	–	Gypsy Council for Education, Culture, Welfare and Civil Rights
GCSE	–	General Certificate of Secondary Education
GNVQ	–	General National Vocational Qualification
HMI	–	Her Majesty's Inspector of schools
JTC	–	Junior Training Centre
LEA	–	Local Education Authority
NATT	–	National Association of Teachers of Travellers
NGEC	–	National Gypsy Education Council
OSCE	–	Organisation for Security and Cooperation in Europe
OFSTED	–	Office for Standards in Education
PER	–	Project on Ethnic Relations
PNEU	–	Parents National Education Union
PSME	–	Personal, Social and Moral Education
STEP	–	Scottish Traveller Education Project
TES	–	Traveller Education Service
TESS	–	Traveller Education Support Service

TOPILOT	–	To OPtimise the Individual Learning of Occupational Travellers
TPW	–	Theatre of Public Works
UN	–	United Nations
YUP	–	Young Unemployed Person

References

Acton, T. (1974) *Gypsy Politics and Social Change*. London: Routledge and Kegan Paul.

Acton, T. (1981) *Surviving Peoples: Gypsies*. London: MacDonald Phoebus Ltd.

Adams, B., Okely, J., Morgan, D. and Smith, D. (1975) *Gypsies and Government Policy in England*. London: Heinemann.

Anisha, B. (1997) *The Declaration of a Lost People*. Wolverhampton: The Partnership Project.

Arnold, T., Franklin, B. and Griffiths, T. (1992) *Bringing Up Children in a Traveller Community*. The Final Report of the West Yorkshire Travellers Project. London: Save the Children.

Binns, D. (1984) *Children's Literature and the Role of the Gypsy*. Manchester: Manchester Travellers' School.

Blaney, B. (1996) 'Travellers "credit" school with flexible friendship.' In B. Jordan (ed.) *Inclusive Education for Secondary Age Travellers*. Edinburgh: STEP at Moray House Institute of Education.

Boswell, S.G. (1970) *The Book of Boswell*. London: Victor Gollancz Ltd.

Braid, D. (1997) 'The construction of identity through narrative folklore and the travelling people of Scotland.' In T. Acton and G. Mundy (eds) *Romani Culture and Gypsy Identity*. Hatfield: University of Hertfordshire Press.

Brearley, M. (1996) *The Roma/Gypsies of Europe: A Persecuted People*. Policy paper for the Institute of Jewish Policy Research. London: Institute of Jewish Policy Research.

Cahn, C. and Trehan, N. (1997) *Time of the Skinheads: Denial and Exclusion of Roma in Slovakia*. Country Reports Series No 3. Budapest: European Roma Rights Center.

Children's Society (1998) *Just Like You*. A video documentary. Bath: Children's Participation Project (Wessex).

Clay, S. (1996) 'Never mind the length – feel the quality.' In B. Jordan (ed.) *Inclusive Education for Secondary Age Travellers*. Edinburgh: STEP at Moray House Institute of Education.

Clay, S. (1997) 'Opening our eyes: Some observations on the attendance of primary aged Traveller pupils registered at schools in a country area of South Wales.' In T. Acton and G. Mundy (eds) *Romani Culture and Gypsy Identity*. Hatfield: University of Hertfordshire Press.

Commission for Racial Equality (1997) *Roots of the Future: Ethnic Diversity in the Making of Britain*. London: Commission for Racial Equality.

Commission of the European Communities (1989) *Resolution of the Council and of the Ministers of Education Meeting with the Council 22nd May 1989 on School Provision for Gypsy and Traveller Children (89/C 153/02)* and *Resolution of the Council and the*

Ministers of Education Meeting with the Council 22nd May 1989 on School Provision for Children of Occupational Travellers (Fairground, Circus and Bargee) (89/C 153/01). Luxembourg: Commission of the European Communities.

Commission of the European Communities (1996) *School Provision for Gypsy and Traveller Children. Report on the Implementation of Measures Envisaged in the Resolution of the Council and of the Ministers of Education Meeting with the Council, 22nd May 1989 (89/C 153/02)*. Luxembourg: Commission of the European Communities.

Cooper, W. (1976) 'The failure of the 1968 Caravan Sites Act.' In *The Romany Guild Looks at the Caravan Sites Act Eight Years On – Who Cares?* London: Romany Guild.

Cripps, Sir J. (1977) *Accommodation for Gypsies.* A report on the working of the Caravan Sites Act 1968. London: HMSO.

Daley, I. and Henderson, J. (eds) (1998) *Static – Life on the Site.* Castleford: Yorkshire Art Circus.

Danaher, P. and Wyer, D. (1996) 'Itinerant education as border pedagogy – the globalisation and localisation of show culture.' In L. Rowan, L. Bartlett and T. Evans (eds) *Shifting Borders – Globalisation, Localisation and Open and Distance Education.* Australia: Deakin University Press.

Danaher, P.A. (ed.) (1998) *Beyond the Ferris Wheel: Educating Queensland Show Children.* Rockhampton: Central Queensland University Press.

Dasanjh, J.S. and Ghuman, P. (1996) *Child-Rearing in Ethnic Minorities.* London: Multilingual Matters Ltd.

Dearling, A. (1998) *No Boundaries: New Travellers on the Road (Outside of England).* Lyme Regis: Enabler Publications.

Department for Education (ed.) (1992) *The Education of Traveller Children.* Report of a seminar organised by the Department of Education and Science, United Kingdom, and the Commission of the European Communities, December 1991. London: DfE.

Department for Education (1993) *Education Act.* London: DfE.

Department for Education and Employment (1994) *School Attendance: Policy and Practice on Categorisation of Absence.* London: DfEE.

Department for Education and Employment (1998) *Are We Missing Out?* A video. London: DfEE.

Department of Education and Science (1944) *Education Act 1944.* London: HMSO.

Department of Education and Science (1967) *Children and their Primary Schools.* The Plowden Report. London: HMSO.

Department of Education and Science (1981) *DES Circular 1/81, Education Act 1980: Admission to Schools, Appeals, Publication of Information and School Attendance Orders.* London: DES.

Department of Education and Science (1983) *The Education of Travellers' Children: An HMI Discussion Paper.* London: DES.

Department of Education and Science (1985) *Education for All, the Report of the Committee of Enquiry into the Education of Children from Ethnic Minority Groups.* The Swann Report. London: HMSO.

Department of Education and Science (1990) *DES Circular 10/90 Education Reform Act 1988: Specific Grant for the Education of Travellers and Displaced Persons. Section 210.* London: DES.

Department of the Environment (1984) *Defining a Gypsy.* London: Gypsy Sites Branch, DoE.

Devon Consortium Traveller Education Service (ed.) (1998) *Get It Sorted.* A teenagers' magazine. Devon: Devon Study Skills Group/EFECOT.

Devon Traveller Education Service (1992) *Making Distance Learning Work: Notes from Experience in the South West.* Plymouth: Devon Traveller Education Service.

Devon Traveller Education Service/Marjon TV (1993) *Between Two Worlds.* A video resource pack (copyright European Commission). Devon: Devon Learning Resources.

Devon Traveller Education Service (1995) *Beyond the Stereotype.* Devon: Devon County Council.

Devon Traveller Education Service (1996) *The Work of the Traveller Education Service.* Devon: Devon County Council.

Dodds, N. (1966) *Gypsies, Didikois and Other Travellers.* London: Johnson Publications.

Doyle, K. (ed.) (1994) 'Romany Routes.' *The Journal of the Romany and Traveller Family History Society* 1, 1.

Duncan, F. (1992) 'The language needs of the young Traveller child.' In P. Pinsent (ed.) *Language, Culture and Young Children.* London: David Fulton Publishers.

EFECOT (1994) 'Efecot Junior, an action programme for and with youngsters.' *EFECOT Journal, Newsline No 10.* p.16–20. Brussels: EFECOT.

EFECOT, Project A4 Steering Committee (1995) *What is your school doing for Travelling Children? – A Guide to Equal Opportunities through Distance Learning.* Brussels: EFECOT.

European Parliament (1995) *Committee on Civil Liberties and Internal Affairs, Consultative Commission on Racism and Xenophobia – Final Report, DOC EN\CM\274\274586.* Brussels: European Parliament.

Evans, K. (1996) 'Right! said Fred.' In B. Jordan (ed.) *Inclusive Education for Secondary Age Travellers.* Edinburgh: STEP at Moray House Institute of Education.

Fonseca, I. (1995) *Bury Me Standing: The Gypsies and their Journey.* New York: Alfred Knopf.

Fraser, Sir A. (1992) *The Peoples of Europe – The Gypsies.* Oxford: Blackwell.

Fraser, P. and Wood, M. (1991) 'Outreach liaison – home-school links.' In *The Education of Traveller Children.* Department of Education and Science, UK and the Commission of the European Communities seminar report. London: DfE.

Gheorghe, N. (1997) 'The social construction of Romani identity.' In T. Acton (ed.) *Gypsy Politics and Traveller Identity.* Hatfield: University of Hertfordshire Press.

Gmelch, G. (1985) *The Irish Tinkers – The Urbanisation of an Itinerant People.* Illinois: Waveland Press Inc.

Godden, R. (1972) *The Diddakoi*. London: Macmillan.

Guardian (1997) 'Cook warns off Gypsies' 28 November.

Hancock, I. (1997) 'Duty and beauty, possession and truth: Lexical impoverishment as control.' In T. Acton and G. Mundy (eds) *Romani Culture and Gypsy Identity*. Hatfield: University of Hertfordshire Press.

Hancock, I., Dowd, S. and Djuric, R. (eds) (1998) *The Roads of the Roma*. Hatfield: University of Hertfordshire Press.

Hawes, D. and Perez, B. (1995) *The Gypsy and the State – The Ethnic Cleansing of British Society*. Bristol: The Policy Press.

HMSO (1994) *The UK's First Report to the UN Committee on the Rights of the Child*. London: HMSO.

Holmes, P. and Jordan, E. (1997) 'The interrupted learner: whose responsibility?' In J. Bastiani (ed.) *Home-school Work in Multicultural Settings*. London: David Fulton Publishers.

Ivatts, A. (1975) *Catch 22 Gypsies – A Report on Secondary Education*. London: ACERT.

Jordan, B. (ed.) (1996) *Inclusive Education for Secondary Age Travellers*. Edinburgh: STEP at Moray House Institute of Education.

Joyce, N. (1985) *Traveller*. A. Farmer (ed.). Dublin: Gill and Macmillan Ltd.

Kaye, G. (1974) *Nowhere to Stop*. London: Penguin.

Kendall, S. (1997) 'Sites of resistance: places on the margin – the Traveller "homeplace".' In T. Acton (ed.) *Gypsy Politics and Traveller Identity*. Hatfield: University of Hertfordshire Press.

Kenny, M. (1997) *The Routes of Resistance: Travellers and Second-Level Schooling*. Aldershot: Ashgate Publishing Limited.

Kenrick, D. and Puxon, G. (1972) *The Destiny of Europe's Gypsies*. London: Chatto-Heinemann for Sussex University Press.

Kenyon, J. (1996) 'Transfer to secondary school – ready, steady, go – /or ready, steady, STOP!!!' In B. Jordan (ed.) *Inclusive Education for Secondary Age Travellers*. Edinburgh: STEP at Moray House Institute of Education.

Kiddle, C. (1981) *What Shall we do with the Children?* Devon: Spindlewood.

Kiddle, C. (1984) Transcripts of interviews with Gypsy Traveller parents. Unpublished. (Extracts included in the text are used with the permission of the interviewees. Some have chosen to remain anonymous.)

Kiddle, C. (1996) 'Representing ourselves: The voice of Traveller children.' In M. John (ed.) *Children in Charge – The Child's Right to a Fair Hearing*. London: Jessica Kingsley Publishers.

Kiddle, C. (1997) Transcripts of interviews with Travellers. Unpublished. (Extracts included in the text are used with the permission of the interviewees. Some have chosen to remain anonymous.)

Lee, K. (1997) 'Australia – sanctuary or cemetery for Romanies?' In T. Acton and G. Mundy (eds) *Romani Culture and Gypsy Identity*. Hatfield: University of Hertfordshire Press.

Lee, T. (1973) *The Romany Guild Looks at the Caravan Sites Act – Five Years After.* London: Romany Guild.

Lee, T. (1976) *The Romany Guild Looks at the Caravan Sites Act Eight Years On – Who Cares?* London: Romany Guild.

Liégeois, J.-P. (1994) *Roma, Gypsies, Travellers.* Strasbourg: Council of Europe Publishing and Documentation Service.

Liégeois, J.-P. (ed.) (1996) 'Towards an encyclopaedia.' *Interface 23*, 10–12. Paris: Centre de recherches tsiganes at the Université René Descartes.

Liégeois, J.-P. and Gheorghe, N. (1995) *Roma/Gypsies: A European Minority.* London: Minority Rights Group.

McColl, E. (1983) *Freeborn Man.* Record album. Beckenham, Kent: Blackthorne Records.

McVeigh, R. (1997) 'Theorising sedentarism: The roots of anti-nomadism.' In T. Acton (ed.) *Gypsy Politics and Traveller Identity.* Hatfield: University of Hertfordshire Press.

Mercer, P. (1991) 'The Traveller experience in education.' In *The Education of Traveller Children: DES/CE Seminar Report.* London: DfE.

Ministry of Housing and Local Government (1960) *Caravan Sites and Control of Development Act.* London: HMSO.

Ministry of Housing and Local Government (1967) *Gypsies and Other Travellers.* London: HMSO.

Ministry of Housing and Local Government (1968) *Caravan Sites Act.* London: HMSO.

Mirga, A. and Gheorghe, N. (1997) *The Roma in the Twenty-First Century: A Policy Paper.* New Jersey: Project on Ethnic Relations.

Naylor, S. and Wild-Smith, K. (1997) *Broadening Horizons, Education and Travelling Children.* Chelmsford: Essex County Council Education.

ní Shuinéar, S. (1997) 'Why do gaujes hate Gypsies so much anyway?' In T. Acton (ed.) *Gypsy Politics and Traveller Identity.* Hatfield: University of Hertfordshire Press.

OFSTED (1996) *The Education of Travelling Children: A Report.* London: OFSTED Publications.

O'Hanlon, C. (1995) *What is your School Doing for Travelling Children? – Staff Development Pack.* Brussels: EFECOT.

Okely, J. (1983) *Changing Cultures: The Traveller-Gypsies.* Cambridge: Cambridge University Press.

Okely, J. (1996) *Own or Other Culture.* London: Routledge.

Okely, J. (1997) 'Cultural ingenuity and travelling autonomy: not copying, just choosing.' In T. Acton and G. Mundy (eds) *Romani Culture and Gypsy Identity.* Hatfield: University of Hertfordshire Press.

Pinsent, P. (ed.) (1992) *Language, Culture and Young Children.* London: David Fulton Publishers.

Plaks, L. (1997) *Preface to Prevention of Violence and Discrimination Against the Roma in Central and Eastern Europe.* A PER Conference Report, Bucharest, March 1997. New Jersey: Project on Ethnic Relations.

Project on Ethnic Relations Report (1992) *The Romanies in Central and Eastern Europe: Illusions and Reality.* Conference report from Stupova, Czechoslavakia, May 1992. New Jersey: Project on Ethnic Relations.

Project on Ethnic Relations Report (1996) *The Media and the Roma in Contemporary Europe: Facts and Fictions.* Conference report from Prague, September 1996. New Jersey: Project on Ethnic Relations.

Project on Ethnic Relations Report (1997) *Prevention of Violence and Discrimination against the Roma in Central and Eastern Europe.* Conference report from Bucharest, Romania, March 1997. New Jersey: Project on Ethnic Relations.

Pullin, R.T. (1985) *Swings and Roundabouts.* Sheffield: Sheffield University.

Puxon, G. (1968) *On the Road.* London: National Council for Civil Liberties.

Refugee Council (1996) *Roma in Eastern Europe and the UK.* Refugee Council factsheet No 19. London: The Refugee Council.

Reid, D. (1992) 'Linguistic diversity and equality.' In P. Pinsent (ed.) *Language, Culture and Young Children.* London: David Fulton Publishers.

Reid, W. (1993) 'Travellers' perspectives.' In B. Jordan (ed.) *Towards an Opening Doors Policy.* Conference report. Edinburgh: Moray House Institute of Education.

Reid, W. (1997a) 'The Traveller and the secondary school: Workshop report.' In B. Forrester (ed.) *Beyond Reading and Writing: Access to Secondary Education for Travellers.* ACERT/Oxford Brookes University European Conference report. Harlow, Essex: ACERT.

Reid, W. (1997b) 'Scottish Gypsies/Travellers and the folklorists.' In T. Acton and G. Mundy (eds) *Romani Culture and Gypsy Identity.* Hatfield: University of Hertfordshire Press.

Reilly, G. (1995) *Moving with the Times.* Devon: Devon County Council.

Reiss, C. (1975) *Education of Travelling Children.* A Schools Council Research Study. London: Macmillan.

Sinclair, O. (1981) *Gypsy Girl.* London: William Collins Sons & Co Ltd.

Singh, J. (1991) 'Educational responses to mobility: Principles and practice.' In *The Education of Traveller Children*, DES/EC seminar report. London: DfE.

Smith, C. (1995) *Not All Wagons and Lanes.* Essex: Essex County Council.

Smith, D. (1997) 'Gypsy aesthetics, identity and creativity: The painted wagon.' In T. Acton and G. Mundy (eds) *Romani Culture and Gypsy Identity.* Hatfield: University of Hertfordshire Press.

Smith, M. (1975) *Gypsies: where now?* Young Fabian Pamphlet 42. London: Fabian Society.

Smith, T. (1997) 'Kaj jekh Rrom zal, savorre Rroma pal lesøe.' *Interface 25*, 18–22.

South West Region Traveller Conference (1996) Case Studies, presented anonymously. Unpublished.

Stevenson, C. (1992) 'Language and learning in the multicultural nursery.' In P. Pinsent (ed.) *Language, Culture and Young Children.* London: David Fulton Publishers.

Tanaka, J. (1997) *Prevention of Violence and Discrimination Against the Roma in Central and Eastern Europe.* PER conference report, Bucharest, March 1997. New Jersey: Project on Ethnic Relations.

UN (1989) *The United Nations Convention on the Rights of the Child.* United Nations General Assembly Official Records, Resolution 25, 44th Session. New York: UN.

Waterson, M. (1997) 'I want more than green leaves for my children – Some developments in Gypsy/Traveller education 1970–96.' In T. Acton and G. Mundy (eds) *Romani Culture and Gypsy Identity.* Hatfield: University of Hertfordshire Press.

Whyte, B (1979) *The Yellow on the Broom.* Great Britain: W. & R. Chambers Ltd.

Williams, D. (1997) Internal Devon Traveller Education Service Report on Video-Conferencing. Unpublished.

Williamson, D. (1983) *Fireside Tales of the Traveller Children.* Edinburgh: Canongate Publishing Ltd.

Wood, M.F. (1973) *In the Life of a Romany Gypsy.* London: Routledge and Kegan Paul.

Wood, M. (1997) 'Home–school work with Traveller children and their families.' In J. Bastiani (ed.) *Home–School Work in Multicultural Settings.* London: David Fulton Publishers.

Worth, J. (1996) 'My God you do look well!' In B. Jordan (ed.) *Inclusive Education for Secondary Age Travellers.* Edinburgh: STEP at Moray House Institute of Education.

Wrexham Traveller Education Service (1997) *Gateway to Success: Secondary School Attendance for Traveller Children.* Handbook from EC/UK research programme under the Socrates programme, Comenius Action II. Wrexham: Wrexham County Borough Council.

Yahwar (1992) A publicity brochure for the theatre group, Yahwar. Sledderlo: Jongeren werking Nieuw Sledderlo.

Subject Index

Author Index

DATE DUE

HIGHSMITH #45230

Over the last twenty-five years there has been an unprecedented expansion of opportunity for Traveller and Gypsy children to attend school. Educational outreach services have developed in parallel with an increased willingness on the part of parents to put their children into school. Cathy Kiddle has studied the effects of this expansion on the lives of the children. Having worked with Travellers and schools for over twenty years, she is well placed to consider the interactions between children, parents and schools. She examines particularly the parent/teacher relationship and the effect this has on the education of the children.

The book looks at education in the context of several distinct travelling groups including Circus, Fairground and New Travellers. While recognising the importance of literacy for their children, many Gypsy Travellers fear that schooling will contribute to the disintegration of their culture, strongly based as it is on family education and supportive kinship networks. Teachers, on the other hand, may have stereotyped ideas of who Gypsies are, and may have their own expectations and demands of children in school. Cathy Kiddle examines the ways in which minority groups are forced to adapt to the changing society around them. She argues that education is important for Traveller children in that it enables them to develop into independent learners and, through this, independent people, able to speak for themselves, make considered choices and act as agents in their own lives. Essentially, her study is optimistic: is parents and teachers are prepared to understand and co-operate with each other, education will help to destroy the marginalisation of Traveller cultures, not the cultures themselves. The children will be able to give their communities a voice for themselves.

Cathy Kiddle first became aware of the issue of education for travelling children while touring with a theatre company in the early 1970s. She began to work with Gypsy and Traveller families in London in 1976, and since then has continued this work as a teacher in Devon. In 1997 she was invited to be a member of the government's Advisory Group on Raising Ethnic Minority Pupil Achievement, and at present she is the co-ordinator of Devon Consortium Traveller Education Service.

Children in Charge
Series Editor: Mary John

The series concentrates on the theme of children's rights, reflecting the increasing knowledge in the area. The perspectives of empowerment and of 'voice' run through the series and the United Nations' Convention on the Right of the Child is used as a benchmark.

Jessica Kingsley *Publishers*
116 Pentonville Road

ISBN 1-85302-684-0

9 781853 026843